An OPUS book

SOCIALISMS
Theories and Practices

Socialisms

Theories and Practices

ANTHONY WRIGHT

Oxford   New York

OXFORD UNIVERSITY PRESS

1986

Oxford University Press, Walton Street, Oxford OX2 6DP
Oxford New York Toronto
Delhi Bombay Calcutta Madras Karachi
Petaling Jaya Singapore Hong Kong Tokyo
Nairobi Dar es Salaam Cape Town
Melbourne Auckland
and associated companies in
Beirut Berlin Ibadan Nicosia

Oxford is a trade mark of Oxford University Press

British Library Cataloguing in Publication Data
Wright, Anthony
Socialisms: theories and practices.——
(An Opus book)
1. Socialism
I. Title
335 HX73
ISBN 0-19-219188-8

Library of Congress Cataloging in Publication Data
Wright, Anthony, 1948-
Socialisms, theories and practices.
(An OPUS book)
Bibliography: p.
Includes index.
1. Socialism. 2. Communism. I. Title. II. Series: OPUS.
HX73.W75 1986 335 86-750
ISBN 0-19-219188-8

Set by Colset Private Ltd.
Printed in Great Britain by
Biddles Ltd.
Guildford and King's Lynn

For Jo, who had a heart, for ever

JOSEPH PHILIP MORYS WRIGHT
13 December 1982–22 August 1985

Nos da, cariad

Preface

The title of this short book is neither a misspelling nor an originality. In setting out to write an introductory essay on socialism that would be accessible to both student and general reader, an approach was needed that could come to terms with the sheer variety of socialism. This variety is organizational and theoretical, historical and contemporary. It has been recognized in one way or another by almost everyone who has engaged with socialism, whether as friend, critic, or observer. However, the response to this recognition has differed.

Some socialists recognize it when they assert the credentials of their particular version of socialism and the illegitimacy of other versions. Some anti-socialists recognize it when they insist on an essentialist description of a nightmare socialism ('the end of all' in Lord Rosebery's phrase) in order to divert attention from the need for a more discriminating approach. It is also recognized by those academic writers on socialism who juggle with definitions and boundary markers in an effort to impose some order on their disorderly material. Others just give up in the face of all this, like the voice heard to exclaim at a Labour Party meeting: 'we don't want practical policies, we want socialist policies!'

In their different ways, all these approaches tend to regard the diversity of socialism as a problem. By contrast, the approach adopted here accepts this diversity as an essential part of what socialism is and has been, and as an important clue to its understanding. This does not mean that it is not possible to draw the boundaries of the socialist 'tradition' so wide that all particular traditions become in some sense part of the same family despite their manifest differences, but what sort of family is it that has, say, both Joseph Stalin and George Orwell among its members? Indeed, surely Orwell's own point in his telling satires, usually misread as attacks on socialism *tout court*, was that there were different *kinds* of socialism and that one (democratic) kind should be embraced and another (authoritarian) kind attacked.

So it is not perversity that prefers to deal less with a singular 'socialism' and more with a plurality of 'socialisms'. The aim is not to classify and label distinct traditions, nor to adopt ready-made labels, but to explore some of the terrain that has provided the materials for different socialist traditions. The chapters that follow focus on aspects of this terrain. First, the diversity of socialist traditions is sketched, along with the variety of socialist arguments. Then four key questions are identified and discussed, relating to the status of the socialist argument (moral value or empirical doctrine?), the means whereby socialist ends are to be achieved (reform or revolution?), the structural form of socialism (statist or associational?), and the leading socialist actors (classes or parties?).

These questions are set within the history of socialist ideas and movements, but they clearly remain as relevant as ever. Finally, against this background, contemporary socialisms are examined and some thoughts on their futures ventured.

Socialism has become an umbrella word, which its friends seek to shelter under (each trying to grab the handle or stab each other with the point) while its enemies wave it around indiscriminately hoping to beat as many opponents on the head as possible. There is no escape from this situation in the search for a 'true' socialism against which particular ideas and movements can be measured and judged. 'Moi, je ne suis pas marxiste' was Marx's famous comment on some of his French followers, while R. H. Tawney remarked on the 'radiant ambiguities' of the word socialism. Such disagreements and tensions are regarded here as the subject-matter of socialism, the basis of divergent traditions. These should be frankly acknowledged, not treated as marginal to an over-arching unity.

Three further points follow from this. Firstly, it will become clear that the dimensions of disagreement discussed here do not always neatly convert into the familiar demarcation lines between socialist traditions (for example, reformist social democracy versus revolutionary communism). Instead, other lines of affiliation and disaffiliation emerge. For example, there are reformist authoritarians (the Webbs, it will be recalled, fell in love with the Soviet Union), just as there are revolutionary libertarians (Rosa Luxemburg). Secondly, to acknowledge a plurality of socialisms is not to embrace the sort of sloppy pluralism that avoids the need for discrimination and judgement. By contrast, by rejecting the notion of a socialism that is historically or theoretically 'correct'

it introduces the need for discrimination between *kinds* of socialism that may be more or less desirable, appropriate, or plausible.

Thirdly, this approach points attention to the extent to which
one socialist tradition (namely 'Marxism') set its face against
such socialist pluralism and endeavoured to secure for itself a
position of organizational and theoretical monopoly. The argument here is that this project was illegitimate, its basis flawed, its
consequences damaging, and that its disintegration is therefore
to be regarded as both necessary and welcome. By extension, this
suggests that one part of the contemporary socialist project
involves a process of unlearning, and that at least some of what
has now to be learnt is to be found in submerged, neglected, and
minority socialist traditions.

One final consideration is also relevant. This is the need for an
approach that can accomodate not merely the evident historical
diversity of socialist movements and ideas, but the actual status
of socialism in the late twentieth-century world. It is a world in
which one person in three lives under a regime that describes itself
as socialist, a fact which bears eloquent testimony to the success
of socialism as a modern ideology, perhaps even *the* modern
ideology. It is, however, also a world in which socialism has
become 'socialism' whenever and wherever socialist regimes have
come to power. In our time socialism ceased to be Left and
became East. The old cry of 'socialism or barbarism' has become
the new reality of socialism *and* barbarism. There is no 'socialist'
society on which socialists would agree in bestowing the label.
These uncomfortable facts must be faced, not least by those
socialists who want to reassert a socialism of emancipation. The
first fact, as G. D. H. Cole announced it a generation ago, is that
'socialism is no longer a single movement, making in a single
direction'.

Acknowledgements

All writing runs up debts and, even if they cannot be repaid, they should at least be acknowledged. I want to mention three in particular, starting with the most general and finishing with the most special.

First, there is the indebtedness of a book like this to the work of all those authors whose scholarship provides the materials out of which its structure and argument is constructed. The fact that it has not generally been possible here to acknowledge such obvious debts individually makes it more necessary that they should be acknowledged collectively. The second debt is owed to the members of my evening class, at the Birmingham and Midland Institute, who spent a lively winter discussing this book with me and in the process contributed a good deal to it. Not for the first time has an adult education class helped to make a book, and for an extramural teacher it is always the most enjoyable debt to be able to record.

Finally, though, by far the greatest influence on me during the writing of this book was the short, magnificent life of the person to whom it is dedicated. He changed everything and everyone he touched. It is really his book.

Contents

1. Traditions

The resulting controversy, between many groups and
tendencies all calling themselves *socialist*, has been long,
intricate and bitter.

Raymond Williams

The history of socialism is the history of socialisms. Moreover, it
is a history not of fraternal plurality, but of rivalry and antagonism. The battle lines have changed (Marxists versus anarchists,
collectivists versus syndicalists, reformers versus revolutionaries,
communists versus social democrats, Trotskyists versus every-
body else . . .), but battle lines there have always been. Many
socialists have reserved their sharpest arrows for attacks on other
socialists, while almost all socialists have found it necessary to
fight on at least two fronts at the same time. The arena of battle
has also changed significantly over time, to take in new places,
contestants, and traditions.

The scene was set when Marx and Engels launched their first
attacks on those early-nineteenth-century socialists they branded
'utopian' (in particular, Saint-Simon, Fourier, and Owen). These
writers, with their 'fanatical and superstitious belief in the
miraculous effects of their social science', were judged to be not
merely irrelevant to the developing class struggle but objectively
reactionary in relation to it. At the same period Marx denounced
the 'amateurism' of the 'French tendencies' (i.e. Proudhon) and
set out to wage war on all such 'idealism' in the name of a scientific class theory. In the mid-1840s, solicited as a correspondent by
Marx, the anarchist socialist Proudhon replied in these terms:

Let us seek together, if you wish, the laws of society, the manner in which
these laws are realised, the process by which we shall succeed in discover-
ing them; but, for God's sake, after having demolished all the *a priori*
dogmatisms, do not let us in our turn dream of indoctrinating the people; do not let us fall into the contradiction of your compatriot Martin
Luther, who, having overthrown Catholic theology, at once set about,
with excommunication and anathema, the foundation of a Protestant

theology. For the last three centuries Germany has been mainly occupied in undoing Luther's shoddy work; do not let us leave humanity with a similar mess to clear up as a result of our efforts. I applaud with all my heart your thought of bringing all opinions to light; let us carry on a good and loyal polemic; let us give the world an example of learned and far-sighted tolerance, but let us not, merely because we are at the head of a movement, make ourselves the leaders of a new intolerance, let us not pose as the apostles of a new religion, even if it be the religion of logic, the religion of reason.

This approach did not commend itself to Marx, nor to the Marxist tradition in general (a fact of some significance in view of the centrality of Marxism in the development of socialism). Socialism was not seen as a mansion with many rooms, but as a house of theory and practice in which dissenting traditions were shown the door in just that spirit of 'excommunication and anathema' of which Proudhon warned.

Marx emphatically and precisely saw the assault on, and defeat of, other available socialist traditions as an essential part of his original project (and a continuing preoccupation). So much so that he began by rejecting even the word 'socialism' because of its prevailing utopian connotations. The word had first appeared in England in the 1820s in an Owenite context, then in French usage in the 1830s. Its origins indicate its resonance. It was used to characterize the schemes of social reconstruction being advanced in England and France at that time by Owen, Saint-Simon, and others, and to describe the adherents of these schemes ('socialists'). In seeking to counter such idealism, Marx needed a political vocabulary that would differentiate his position and distance it from these prevailing socialisms. Hence, in 1848, the world was presented not with the socialist but the *Communist Manifesto*. At this period the word 'communist' was associated with a more abrasive tradition, revolutionary, egalitarian, and proletarian, as exemplified by Babeuf and the left wing of the French Revolution.

It was this tradition, of revolutionary class action, that Marx wanted to draw upon in opposition to the prevailing varieties of 'socialism'. Looking back forty years later, Engels wrote that: 'We could not have called it a *Socialist* manifesto. In 1847, Socialism was a middle-class movement, Communism a working-class movement. Socialism was, on the continent at least, respectable; Communism was the very opposite.' Even in subsequent years, when usage had changed and blurred, it seems that Marx always retained a certain antipathy to 'socialism' as both word and concept (reflected in its pejorative appearances in *Capital*, usually referring to Proudhon and the utopians). However, as the nineteenth century progressed, socialism established itself as the general word and Marxism increasingly established its proprietorship over it.

Having entered this linguistic minefield, some further cautious exploration is appropriate. The diversity of socialist traditions has been reflected in the variety of socialist usage, and in the shifts in usage over time. Even when the linguistic ascendancy of 'socialism' was established, wrested by the Marxists from the utopians and the anarchists, 'communism' retained a variety of usages both old and new. For example, it was preferred by William Morris because it carried a traditional meaning of revolutionary class action to secure property in common. In England, at least, this served to distinguish it from Fabian 'socialism' in the 1880s and 1890s. The word could also refer to an original or primitive communism before class society, while it developed a further and more familiar meaning as a future, higher stage of social development beyond the socialism that would be the immediate successor to class society. It was launched on a new lease of life when, in 1918, the Bolsheviks appropriated it to mark their split from an allegedly degenerate European socialism and to claim an authentic historical pedigree. From that moment communism became Communism, and it was difficult thereafter to retrieve its other usages.

Matters were made no clearer by the fact that in becoming Communists the Bolsheviks and their satellite parties did not relinquish their claim to be 'socialists' but instead now claimed to be the only authentic socialists. They sought to wrest any title to the name from the European socialist tradition that had called itself Social Democratic in the late nineteenth and early twentieth centuries as it combined its Marxist doctrine with party organization. In Europe, before 1914, 'social democracy' meant organized Marxism; after 1917, it came to mean organized reformism. The Communists, appropriating Marx, not only denied the socialist credentials of social democracy, but attacked it (at one period as 'social fascism') as essentially reactionary and counter-revolutionary. Some socialists responded to these developments by coining the term 'democratic socialism' to describe a position that was non-Communist and critical of undemocratic socialism as practised by the Bolsheviks, but at the same time was not merely reformist or ameliorative but remained committed to the reorganization of society on a socialist basis. This was a difficult position to sustain, but the need for it was a reflection of the fragmentation of socialism that had taken place. In a sense, democratic socialists were social democrats who meant it. A further linguistic footnote was provided by those social democrats in Britain who, in the early 1980s, became Social Democrats. Intended to signify their affiliations with a wider tradition, this change was also interpreted as an attempt to convert social democracy from a tradition *within* European socialism to a position outside and in opposition to it.

This excursion into the political language of socialism has raised many issues that will require further consideration later. For the moment, though, it is sufficient to record that the variety of socialisms is amply reflected in the varieties of socialist usage. This also serves as a reminder of those developments that have contributed to the evolution of socialism. For example, Marx's early antipathy towards 'socialism' is a reminder that there was socialism before Marx (just as there have remained socialisms alongside and outside Marxism). The point here is not to play the familiar game of ransacking history for the precursors of socialism, from Thomas More to Plato and beyond, but to register the fact that the development of socialism has usually been viewed through the prism of the theoretical supremacy of Marx and the organizational dominance of Marxism.

This is especially the case with the 'utopian' socialists, traditionally dismissed by the Marxist tradition for their inferiority to the 'scientific socialism' that was developed by Marx and Engels. Indeed, the terms of this dismissal are such that it seems that the historical *function* of the utopians is to be superseded by Marxism. Yet the work of these early-nineteenth-century writers retains interest and significance, and does contribute to later socialist traditions. This is true of Owen's vision of social harmony through co-operation, of Fourier's scheme for community production that would nourish individuality rather than repress it, of Saint-Simon's plan for the reorganization of the social and economic order, and of Proudhon's mutualism that represented a form of decentralized producer democracy. When all the usual criticisms are made (that Saint-Simon did not mention capitalism, that Fourier was dotty, that Proudhon was full of contradictions, etc.), and when the obvious theoretical inferiority of these writers to Marx is acknowledged (as it was by Marx), the fact remains that they did represent the first intellectual challenge to industrial capitalism and its ideology of liberal individualism, and did build a bridge to later socialist traditions.

Thus Proudhon nourished an anti-collectivist tradition, Owen a co-operative tradition, Fourier a libertarian tradition, and Saint-Simon a technocratic tradition. This indicates how misleading it is simply to dub them 'utopian', thereby suggesting a uniformity instead of the diversity of these early-nineteenth-century socialisms. For Marx, however, they were essentially the same: not, as is usually suggested, because they could not say who was to bring about social change nor how they were to do it, but because they fundamentally misunderstood the nature of the social process. The lack of an agency was a reflection of this, as was their proclivity to indulge in moral appeals and undertake experiments in communal living. By contrast, Marx offered an account of the social process in which theory and practice were united and morality merged with necessity. Historical development was to be explained in terms of material forces which gave rise to forms of class society. Its present form was capitalism, or bourgeois society, a system of exploitation that operated through the extraction of surplus value from wage labourers. However, in creating a proletariat, capitalism had also created the agency whereby it would itself be transcended. The revolutionary victory of this exploited class, a particular class that was also a 'universal' class because it was the carrier of a general liberation, would mark the end of class society and the rediscovery by humanity of its essential (but previously estranged) species-being. Against such a prospectus, the offerings of the 'utopian' socialists could indeed seem rather paltry.

If there were socialist traditions before Marxism (or the foundations for such traditions), there were also socialisms alongside Marxism during the nineteenth century. Again, the tendency has been to view these traditions from the perspective of a Marxism that had consolidated its hold on European socialism by the final quarter of the century. Thus the progress of Marxism is charted in terms of Marx's intellectual victories over Lassalle, or political victories over Bakunin. Yet this obscures the extent to which a socialist tradition of state action in the conditions of a widening franchise (for example, associated with Louis Blanc in France and with Lassalle in Germany) was taking shape from the middle of the nineteenth century, and was not born in a later 'revisionism'. Similarly, Marx's contest with the anarchist Bakunin in the First International is sometimes presented by orthodox Marxists as an irritating distraction from the historic march of 'scientific socialism', instead of evidence of the continuing appeal of a non-collectivist tradition that had been associated with Proudhon ('the master of us all' according to Bakunin) and was to be taken up by anarchist communists like Kropotkin and by the syndicalists. There was also an insurrectionary tradition, linked with the name of Blanqui, that saw revolution not as the movement of a class but the work of a conspiratorial élite of professional revolutionaries. Lenin was to provide a reminder of this tradition.

It is against this complex background that the ascendancy of Marxism within European socialism should be seen. This ascendancy was secured when, from the 1870s, socialism became both theory and movement with the development of workers' organizations in the main European countries. Because of its theoretical sweep, and the role it assigned to working-class political action, Marxism was well placed to provide the ideological underpinning of workers' parties. This was precisely the role that it did play during the period of the Second International from the late 1880s through to 1914. In the words of George Lichtheim, distinguished historian of socialism, Marxism 'functioned as an integrative ideology' in these years. However, it would be misleading to regard this apparent integration as evidence that the variety of socialist traditions had at last been reduced to unitary form. The attempt was made to make Marxism perform this function; but the attempt failed.

The need for an integrative ideology was apparent to any observer of European socialism in the 1880s. Three main traditions were in evidence. There was Marxism, now organized as 'social democracy'. There was anarchism, and its anarcho-syndicalist derivatives. There was also reformism, most explicitly seen in English Fabianism but evident too in the democratic collectivism espoused by the 'possibilists' in France, headed by Paul Brousse. Thus the Second International was born out of two rival congresses convened simultaneously in Paris in 1889, by the Marxists and the possibilists (the latter were even alleged to have waylaid provincial delegates at the railway station and misdirected them to their own congress). The anarchists meanwhile devoted their considerable energies to causing disturbances at both of these congresses. The engine of the Second International was the German Social Democratic Party, which had itself been formed at a unity congress between the German socialists in 1875 at Gotha and had later adopted a thoroughgoing Marxist programme at Erfurt in 1891. This German party, led by Bebel and Liebknecht, then set about making the Second International in its own image.

It should be noted that socialism's centre of gravity, originally to be located in France and England, had now shifted decisively eastwards, to Germany. The Germans had created a united party and, in the face of the anti-socialist laws, had constructed an impressive organization and a mass following. By 1890 the party had won the support of about a fifth of the German electorate. Its prestige was enhanced by the traditional association of its leaders with Marx (until his death in 1883) and Engels (who lived on until 1895). It is not surprising that socialists elsewhere endeavoured to emulate the Germans by setting up their own Social Democratic parties, or that the Germans were the driving force of the Second International. They led the struggle against the anarchists ('anarchism' had now become the catch-all category to describe all disbelievers in a disciplined party equipped with a 'scientific' doctrine), and anarchist ideas were finally purged from the International in 1896. The Germans also endeavoured through the International to impose some unity on socialism in France, where the variety of socialist traditions was still much in evidence. The French Marxists, led by Guesde and organized since 1879 in the *Parti Ouvrier Français*, found themselves opposed on two socialist fronts by the syndicalists and the possibilists (as well as other independent groupings on the Left). These differences within French socialism kept spilling over into the International, an embarrassing reminder of socialist disunity.

Just as the German Marxists had dispatched the anarchists,

they finally managed to discipline the French socialists. At the 1904 congress of the International, in many ways its high-water mark, the 'revisionists' (notably Bernstein), who wanted to adjust both the economic and political analysis of Marxism in the light of changing circumstances, were roundly condemned and traditional doctrine reaffirmed. This position was then imposed on the member parties of the International and the French socialists were called upon to unite on this basis. This they did when Jaurès, socialist idealist and outstanding leader of French socialism until his assassination in 1914, agreed to bring his members into the new party, the name of which (*Section Française de l'Internationale Ouvrière*, SFIO) was a reminder of its origins. Thus French socialism was formally united from outside, an expression of the dominant position of German social democracy within European socialism and of its ability to impose an organizational model and doctrinal basis on the international movement. In turn, this enabled the International to engage in impressive displays of solidarity against bourgeois nationalism and war and in affirmations of international proletarian brotherhood. European socialism seemed to have forged a unity out of its divergent traditions, courtesy of the German social democrats. Moreover, this unity seemed to be rooted in a secure theoretical position.

This security was provided by 'Marxism'. The inverted commas are necessary here to indicate the role played by this body of doctrine during the Second International period. It should be recalled that the term 'Marxist' (and its variants) was originally deployed as a form of sectarian abuse against 'Marx's party' by Bakunin and his followers, a reply in kind to the language of sectarian vilification ('Proudhonism', 'Bakuninist', etc.) that Marx himself had developed and deployed. Gradually, however, the term lost its negative, sectarian connotations and assumed a more positive orientation. The publication of the first volume of *Capital* in 1867 extended Marx's authority within European socialism, as did his role in the production of the basic documents of the International Working Men's Association (First International). The dramatic, if brief, revolutionary events of the Paris Commune in 1871 also had the effect of promoting Marx's reputation outside socialist circles. Thus in the period between the First and Second Internationals the ideas of Marx and Engels became recognized as the basis of 'scientific socialism', of which they were the acknowledged founders. Their work now provided the reference point for socialist argument within and between different traditions, just as it also reshaped the conceptual vocabulary of socialism.

This extending influence provided the basis for the mobilization of 'Marxism' as an integrative ideology by the Marxist element of German social democracy. It was not enough that the ideas of Marx should gradually be assimilated by the various schools of European socialism, but that Marxism-as-system should be established as the unitary doctrine of the international socialist movement. So 'Marxism' was marshalled into this role of official doctrine, an assertion of theoretical supremacy described (by the historian Georges Haupt) as 'this process of hegemonization'. This entailed an emphasis on its scientific status and completeness. The leading figure in this assertion of the ideological hegemony of Marxism was Karl Kautsky, theoretician-in-chief of German social democracy and dubbed the 'pope of Marxism', who deployed it against what he described as the prevailing 'eclectic socialism' (composed of elements from Marx, Lassalle, Bakunin, Proudhon, Rodbertus, etc.). The theoretical victory of Marxism would eradicate such eclecticism, and would also ensure the political victory of the Marxists. This process was encouraged by Engels, and the 'dialectical' materialism developed in his polemic against the materialist philosopher Dühring (*Anti-Dühring*) contributed greatly to the promotion of Marxism as a system. As a system, it was a self-contained proletarian science, and as such gave an intellectual backing to the social democratic political stance of separateness from the institutions of bourgeois society.

It was in this context that 'Marxism' functioned as the ideological underpinning of the Second International. It was deliberately employed in this way by the German Marxists, initially within German social democracy and then internationally. It was used to turn socialism into a unitary tradition, securely anchored in a body of scientific doctrine bequeathed by its undisputed founding fathers. Other traditions could be attacked in its name and their adherents brought to heel. Bridges could be built to it from more distant traditions, such as that elaborately constructed by Plekhanov from Russian populism. It was all very impressive. It was also a sham. Dissenting traditions were not subsumed or subjugated, either by Marxist science or by political muscle.

This was evident in the resurgence of syndicalism that unsettled the ranks of social democracy in the late nineteenth and early twentieth centuries. Even in England, Beatrice Webb could note in her diary in 1912 that: 'Syndicalism has taken the place of the old-fashioned Marxism. The angry youth, with bad complexion, frowning brow and weedy figure is nowadays a Syndicalist; the glib young workman whose tongue runs away with him today mouths the phrases of French Syndicalism, instead of those of German Social Democracy.' Similarly, despite the denunciation of 'revisionism' and the assertion of Marxist orthodoxy by the Second International, reformist tendencies had not in fact been suppressed either theoretically or practically. The revisionists had shattered the notion of a single, uncontestable 'Marxism' at the level of theory, while the political practice of the orthodox was opening up a widening gulf between revolutionary theory and the actual business of social democratic politics. The period of the Second International has been called the golden age of Marxism. It was also the period when what Marx merely described as his theory of 'critical materialist socialism' was converted into 'Marxism' and presented as the complete theory of a unitary socialism. In fact, there remained other theories and a plurality of socialisms; and what seemed like an extension of Marx's ideas into a system really involved their contraction. Much of this was to become painfully clear in 1914 and subsequently.

However, even in the years before 1914 it was already apparent that the Second International did not encompass all available socialisms, and that it was possible to be a socialist without also being a Marxist. It is true that in Europe as a whole most socialists were now Marxists, but this did not prevent many of them from interpreting the term in ways consistent with other traditions. In Britain, however, socialist traditions had developed since the 1880s that were non-Marxist and therefore distinctive from the perspective of European socialism as a whole. The revival of socialism in Britain in the early 1880s, after the long interlude following the collapse of Chartism, certainly took the form initially of an attempt (led by Hyndman) to establish a Social Democratic party on the German model with a Marxist basis. The maturity of industrial capitalism in Britain, its large and increasingly organized working class, and the long residence here of Marx and Engels, might be thought to have augured well for this attempt. Yet it failed, largely because of the developing force of other domestic traditions. Thus William Morris sought to integrate Marxist ideas with a Ruskinian tradition of aesthetic protest against the 'civilization' of commercial capitalism. Other anti-capitalist (though non-socialist) literary and cultural traditions were drawn upon in the development of an ethical socialism, involving a moral critique of capitalism and the presentation of socialism as a project for the remoralization of society. An ethical socialism of this kind, which came to be associated in particular with the Independent Labour Party founded in 1893, and was expressed by its leading figures, such as Keir Hardie and Robert Blatchford, became a dominant element in the ideology of British socialism. It was non-Marxist without also being anti-Marxist, in the sense that it was willing to acknowledge the importance of 'scientific' socialism even though the essential socialist case was a moral one (and this did involve a rejection of the class theory of Marxism).

Ethical socialism was reformist, in terms of means though not of ends. However, the main school of British reformist socialism was Fabianism, the product of a small group of thinkers and writers (amongst whom Sidney Webb and Bernard Shaw were pre-eminent) who had founded the Fabian Society in 1884 and equipped it with a doctrine of gradualist collectivism, a doctrine that made its first major public appearance in 1889, in the famous collection of *Fabian Essays*. Fabianism was constructed out of an assortment of intellectual ingredients, notably from the nineteenth-century doctrines of positivism and utilitarianism, and out of the politics of advanced radicalism. It was not merely non-Marxist but anti-Marxist, in the sense that it challenged the basis of Marx's economic analysis and claimed to have developed a superior account of the nature of capitalist exploitation, and in the sense that it rejected Marxism's strategy of revolutionary class action as wholly inappropriate to English conditions. Fabianism offered a strategy of 'resolute constitutionalism' (Shaw's phrase) that would increasingly capture the state, both centrally and locally, for collectivist purposes. This strategy was buttressed by a historical analysis that showed this process to be already well underway and the forces of individualism on the run. So here was a reformist tradition that stood at odds with the mainstream of European socialism before 1914, although it seems to have exercised some influence on the development of Bernstein's revisionism during his period of London exile. According to Rosa Luxemburg, Bernstein (whose *Evolutionary Socialism* became a classic text of socialist reformism) 'constructed his theory upon relationships obtaining in England. He sees the world through English spectacles.'

English exceptionalism was to be ended in 1914, but so was much else besides. The collapse of the Second International was the end of an illusion, or rather several. When the German, French, and Austrian socialists responded to the patriotic call in 1914 and voted for war credits this not only killed the International but also the illusion of international proletarian solidarity. It shattered the illusion of social democracy as an independent force outside the institutions of bourgeois states. It revealed the illusion of a unitary socialism, both internationally and theoretically. It exposed the gulf between Marxist theory and social democratic practice. Above all, perhaps, it not only ended an era in the history of socialism but inaugurated a new era in which all socialist traditions were to be profoundly transformed. In the words of James Joll, a historian of the Second International, 'the Socialist world was never to be the same again after 1914'. Kolakowski extends the point: 'The summer of 1914 saw the beginning of a process whose consequences are still with us, and whose final outcome cannot be foreseen.'

In socialist terms, the war began with the collapse of socialist internationalism and ended with the Bolshevik revolution in Russia. 'Overwhelmed by opportunism the Second International had died. Down with opportunism and long live the Third International!' Lenin's response to the events of 1914 marked the beginning of a formal rupture within socialism, a rupture that has dominated its subsequent history. It was a rupture that Lenin deliberately engineered, as he insisted that what had been revealed was the degeneracy of the whole pre-1914 social democratic tradition. This had preached Marxism, but practised reformism. This had claimed to stand apart from bourgeois society, but had thrown in its lot with that society at the moment of test. Of course, Lenin was right about all of this, but this is less significant than the conclusions he drew from the indictment. One reasonable conclusion that might have suggested itself was the need to amend theory in the direction of practice, but this was not likely to commend itself to Lenin as he organized the Bolsheviks for revolution in Russia. Instead he sought to make Bolshevism the centre of a new, authentic revolutionary tradition that would integrate Marxist theory and practice and provide a rallying point for all those socialist elements who rejected reformism and were committed to the international class struggle.

The victory of the Bolsheviks in Russia turned this from a doctrinal position into an organizational project. It was a project that was to split the ranks of socialists everywhere, and to compress the variety of socialist traditions into two antagonistic camps. The major socialist tradition, Marxism, was appropriated as the official ideology of a regime, an elevation sealing it off for more than a generation as a living source of socialist ideas. During the period of the Second International, Marxism had at least functioned as an open orthodoxy, with no coercive power over heretics, which had to sustain itself in argument conducted at an impressive theoretical level. It was now destined to function as a closed orthodoxy, with its official interpreters, who could sustain their interpretations through their command of the machinery of a totalitarian state. Some socialists in Europe, notably the Austro-Marxists, endeavoured to maintain a Marxist position that was independent of Leninism, but this remained a minority enterprise in a hostile political environment. Marxism had become Marxism-Leninism, with few prepared to quarrel about the hyphen.

Other departures in nomenclature identified the rupture within socialism that took place in the decade after 1914. After seizing power, Lenin's party signalled their repudiation of 'social democracy' by adopting the title of 'Communist' in 1918. In that year the Russian Social-Democratic Labour Party (Bolsheviks) renamed itself as the Communist Party of the Soviet Union (Bolsheviks). It was the assertion of a historical pedigree in Marxist terms and a distancing from the social democracy of the Second International. One of the celebrated Twenty-One Conditions governing admission of parties to the new Communist

(Third) International, adopted in 1920, made this abundantly clear. Member parties would have to take the label 'Communist', and far from being a point of detail this was 'a political one of great importance'. In the words of the document: 'The Communist International has declared a decisive war against the entire bourgeois world and all the yellow, social democratic parties. Every rank-and-file worker must clearly understand the difference between the communist parties and the old official "social democratic" or "socialist" parties which have betrayed the cause of the working class.'

It is almost impossible to exaggerate the significance of what happened between 1914 and 1924. In the period before 1914 the socialist world did, with some exceptions and dissenting voices, achieve at least the appearance of organizational and theoretical unity. During the decade after 1914 this was converted into organizational and doctrinal warfare between two rival camps. Communist parties were licensed in Moscow by the Third International to wage war on non-Communist socialist parties throughout the world. The reconstruction of a Socialist International in 1923 in response to this was an acknowledgement of the permanent nature of the split that had taken place. Socialism was polarized between communism and social democracy, each claiming a unique socialist legitimacy. However, if the pre-1914 attempt to create a unitary socialist tradition had broken down, the subsequent compression of socialist traditions into the two organized camps of official communism and official social democracy was no less inadequate. It left no room for an independent Left that was nourished by traditions unsympathetic both to a communism that was authoritarian and to a social democracy that, partly in response to the communist challenge, had moved further in the direction of mere reformism. The brief attempt in 1920 by an assorted group of non-aligned socialists to organize a socialist 'centre' between parliamentarism and Bolshevism (in the so-called 'Two-and-a-Half International') had failed. It was not really the case that there were just two socialist traditions, which could be organized into rival armies, but for a long time it did seem so. This was, incidentally, also the time when fascism was able to make its malevolent advance.

This brief sketch clearly does not exhaust the significance of the developments it describes. There also took place a fundamental shift in what may be called the geography of socialism, with far-reaching implications. The socialist centre of gravity shifted eastwards during the nineteenth century, from England and France to Germany, and with the Bolshevik capture of power in Russia it moved still further east in the early twentieth century. However, this geographical movement also represented a dramatic break with many of the leading assumptions of pre-1914 socialism. These assumptions were economic, social, and cultural. Their combined implication was that socialism would succeed capitalism in those countries that had a mature capitalist economy, with a developed class structure, and that socialism would inherit and extend the democratic machinery and cultural capital of such societies. The success of Bolshevism challenged all of these assumptions, which is why so much theoretical ingenuity was employed by the communists to accommodate what had happened in terms of Marxist doctrine and to integrate it into a general prospectus for world revolution that would encompass the heartlands of industrial capitalism. The collapse of that prospectus was to require still further ingenuity in doctrine in an increasingly convoluted attempt to keep up with the shifting demands of domestic and international policy.

However, the changed geography of socialism did not present problems merely for the communist tradition. The non-communist, social democratic and democratic socialist traditions were now presented with a world in which socialism was no longer merely a theoretical and organizational project but the self-description of an actual regime. Further, this was a regime which, apart from its replacement of private by public property, seemed not merely to lack but positively to outlaw the democratic rights and individual freedoms that had always been promised, indeed assumed, as an essential part of the socialist project. Thus, from 1917, social democrats and democratic socialists have had to pursue their version of socialism in an environment in which 'actually existing socialism' has meant something else. This has had a profoundly damaging effect on socialist fortunes in Europe and beyond, and has provided invaluable ammunition for the opponents of socialism in the propaganda battle for electoral support. In this sense, as Isaac Deutscher has remarked, the Russian Revolution 'has acted as a deterrent to revolution in the West'.

A further shift in socialist geography also took place. If communism pulled the socialist centre of gravity eastwards, the contrary pull exercised by the social democratic tradition now located itself in western and northern Europe, notably in Britain and Scandinavia. Thus Britain, which stood outside the main current of European socialism during the period of the Second International before 1914, became from the 1920s a leading representative of the non-communist socialist tradition. Meanwhile, anarchist traditions survived in southern Europe, especially in Spain. Behind this geographical fracture, there lurked a larger question or rather a cluster of related questions. Perhaps the idea of a single socialism was not merely historically or theoretically flawed, but culturally inadequate. Instead of a universalist socialism, experience seemed to suggest that there could be different sorts of socialism just as there were different sorts of societies.

Russia showed that there could be a socialism, defined in terms of strategy and form of rule, in societies without mature capitalist economies, large working classes, and developed political institutions. Equally, the social democratic strength in those countries of western Europe which were stable capitalist democracies seemed to suggest that a socialism of another kind also required a particular cultural base. Of course, one response to such lines of thought has been to deny the legitimacy of some kinds of socialism. Thus the Soviet Union is said, by some socialists, to be not 'really' a socialist country; and social democratic parties are also said, by other socialists (or sometimes the same ones), to be not 'really' socialist at all. Another response to the same difficulty, on the part of some socialists, has been to accept the legitimacy of all parties and regimes describing themselves as socialist, despite their manifest differences, because, in a fundamental sense, all socialists are necessarily on the same side. Both of these responses, though very different, share a common attachment to a unitary view of socialism. In other words, while they differ on what socialism consists of, taking a sectarian or catholic view of the matter, they both agree that there is *something*, in the singular, that socialism is. To challenge this is not to relapse into the sort of disabling relativism that suspends all critical judgement, but it is to insist from the evidence that there are demonstrably different *kinds* of socialism, which seem broadly to correspond to different kinds of societies. This was evident, at the level of doctrine, before 1914; and it has been given ample practical demonstration since 1917.

The need to think in terms of a variety of socialisms reflecting different national and cultural environments was argued even before 1914 by the Austro-Marxist, Otto Bauer. Of course, the national dimension of socialism was a matter of more than passing interest to a socialist in the multinational Austro-Hungarian empire, but Bauer's argument that 'the cultural character of each nation stamps itself on its socialism' had general application. One of its implications, as Bauer himself wanted to point out, was that different national traditions should be allowed to pursue their own kind of socialism in their own way. Intended originally as a contribution to the pre-1914 debates within Marxism on the 'national question', it was to become of more pressing practical significance later. The new Soviet state soon revealed in the repressive treatment of its own nationalities what Lenin's theoretical discussion of national autonomy actually amounted to. Equally, the communist Third International (Comintern) rejected in both its doctrine and its practice any notion of there being a plurality of socialisms as it enforced its own Moscow model on the communist parties that it controlled. In the memorable phrase of Léon Blum, heir of Jaurès and leader of French socialism between the wars, the French Communist Party was '*un parti nationaliste étranger*'. The irony, of course, was that the Soviet Union was itself a monument to the impact of national traditions on the form that socialism had taken (or, as the Russian poet put it, 'Peter the Great was the first Bolshevik').

In the post-1945 world, considerations of this kind assumed new interest and importance. On the one hand, in western Europe the social democratic parties moved further towards reformism and a permanent accommodation with liberal capitalism, in response to what were perceived as the social and economic changes taking place in these societies. The clearest formal signal of this accommodation was the adoption of the Bad Godesberg programme by the German Social Democrats in 1959. More recently, the adoption of a 'Eurocommunist' perspective by the leading communist parties in western Europe, involving a new polycentrism in their relations with Moscow, also represents a form of accommodation with the 'national' traditions within which they operate (exactly what else it represents remains to be seen). The events of 1968, that *annus mirabilis* of post-war radicalism, meanwhile confronted the communist parties with their worst fears about being outflanked on the Left. More dramatically, outside Europe, there have been new socialist regimes and new socialist movements. Many of these, from Maoism to 'African socialism', have wanted to emphasize the national and cultural particularity of their traditions. They have needed to do this, partly to fit the facts, but also because of the evident distance of their experience from some of the central assumptions of classical western socialism (in terms of economic development, class structure, nationalism, and much else besides). Not surprisingly, perhaps, those reared in classical Marxism often react dismissively to the 'Marxism' of Third World socialisms (thus Maoism is an 'infantile parody' of Leninism to Lichtheim, and 'childish' to Kolakowski). Though doubtless justified, their reaction further points the need to think in terms of a plurality of 'socialisms' rather than a single model.

It should be said again that this does not mean an indiscriminating relativism. It does involve some relativism, in so far as it allows that some forms of socialism may be more appropriate to certain types of society (for example, that democratic socialism is tied to the developed capitalist democracies, or that—in Baran's words—'socialism in backward and underdeveloped countries has a powerful tendency to become a backward and underdeveloped socialism'). This does not avoid discrimination, though, since the fact that a certain kind of socialism may be more or less appropriate to a particular society does not thereby make it more or less desirable or worthy of support. The sort of socialism to be found in the Soviet Union may be highly appropriate in terms of that society (as is often argued), but this does not make it any less tyrannical or more deserving of support from democratic socialists. The world is full of socialisms. There is no unitary tradition. On one view, this represents a process of theoretical disintegration. On a different view, however, it is a reminder that socialism has always been distinguished by its diversity. During the long period, intensified by the Cold War, when this diversity was compressed into the two opposing blocs of official communism and official social democracy, this could be forgotten. It now reappears, along with the sort of traditions that sustained it.

2. Arguments

Socialism, however, is obviously a word with more than one meaning.

R. H. Tawney

The diversity of socialist traditions has been reflected in the variety of socialist arguments. The familiar question 'what is socialism?' therefore requires a less familiar answer. If there is not a single socialist tradition but a plurality of traditions, then the ideas and arguments associated with these traditions have to be discussed in similarly plural terms. So the question should more properly be asked as: 'what are the ideas and arguments of what kinds of socialisms?'

There is no shortage of available definitions of what socialism is, but there is a shortage of agreed definitions. Indeed, how could it be otherwise? Much harmless fun may be had in definition swapping, as long as there is no expectation that this will yield a form of words that encompasses the variety of the thing described. What is possible, of course, is to define the characteristics of a particular kind of socialism, existing or aspirational, preferred or disparaged, but this is a different enterprise (though often passed off as the same). Thus it may be possible to define 'democratic socialism' in terms of certain essential characteristics, although the adjective indicates an initial act of differentiation and the terms of the resulting definition are likely to leave many open spaces at the level of policy and practice (where it matters). Still, it is both possible and desirable that such limited and limiting definitions are essayed, in order to clarify what is being described, defended, or attacked, but on the understanding that what is being discussed is a particular kind of socialism and not the attempted appropriation of the whole range of socialist traditions.

Consider the following definitions of socialism, quickly culled from a shelf of socialist literature old and new. It is tempting to include Lenin's 'soviet power plus electrification', and Herbert Morrison's 'what a Labour government does', as the authentic viewpoint of organizational socialism (a strange coupling, of Lenin and Morrison, even turns out on this view to be rather less strange than it seems), but the temptation should perhaps be resisted. The following remain, all attempting to define what socialism essentially consists of:

The condition of common ownership and control of the means of production, or at least an important part of the means of production, exercised at least putatively on behalf of the whole people without respect for special privileges, and at least putatively in compliance with their decisions. *Charles Taylor*

A society is to that extent socialist in which it provides the possibilities for a free creative development of every individual. *Gajo Petrović*

Equal division of the national income among all the inhabitants of the country, and the maintenance of that equal division as the invariable social postulate, the very root of the Constitution. *Bernard Shaw*

An institutional pattern in which the control over means of production and over production itself is vested with a central authority—or, as we may say, in which, as a matter of principle, the economic affairs of society belong to the public and not the private sphere. *Joseph Schumpeter*

A social order in which there is the maximum feasible equality of access, for all human beings, to economic resources, to knowledge, and to political power, and the minimum possible domination exercised by any individual or social group over any others. *Tom Bottomore*

A social order founded on more social and economic equality, higher social and economic security, and greater emphasis on community values than are produced by the spontaneous development of an industrial economy under the profit motive. *Richard Lowenthal*

The dominance of social ownership in the economy, together with political and economic democracy. *Alec Nove*

The greatest possible degree of conscious human control over the personal, social and natural environment exercised democratically. *Gavin Kitching*

Even this brief and random definitional excursion well illustrates the difficulties involved in the attempt to pin socialism down. None of the definitions here acknowledges that it refers to a particular version of socialism, yet some manifestly do, as is evident from their elaborate conditioning clauses. The frequent emphasis on democracy makes this clear, for what these authors want is to distinguish their 'democratic' socialism from both the theory and practice of undemocratic socialism. But, as George Lichtheim has put it: 'One can have democracy without socialism, and vice versa. Whether the two can be effectively combined is the prime question of our age.' This question should not be ducked by pretending that democratic socialism is by definition the only 'true' socialism when it obviously is not.

A secure refuge from such problems might be thought to be found in the assertion that socialism is essentially about the public ownership of the means of production, whatever else it might also be about. Yet this too is clearly inadequate, certainly if offered as a root definition. Partly, this is because socialists have disagreed about both the importance and extent of public ownership; but too, because a system of public ownership may well also be inegalitarian and undemocratic and therefore a denial of what many socialists would want to regard (*pace* Lichtheim) as basic socialist objectives. There is the further difficulty that public ownership may be centralist (as Schumpeter insists it has to be), although this is a conclusion that would be resisted by socialist traditions that are decentralist and libertarian.

A more promising path would seem to be that offered by attempts to define basic socialist values (such as equality) and then to give effect to these values in terms of structures and procedures (such as public ownership). In other words, we should first define socialism by its values or goals, then explore the appropriate means whereby such ends might be realized or advanced. Yet this approach would be rejected by those socialists for whom values have no independent status outside particular modes of production and who hold that the establishment of a socialist mode of production is the precondition for the realization of socialist (i.e. universal, non-class) values. Socialists of this kind, as will be seen, tend to dismiss a socialist moralism that deals in the language of justice and equality as so much *petit bourgeois* distraction. Even if this dismissal is disallowed, a socialism of values still faces formidable difficulties in achieving definitional coherence and a distinctive identity. For example, socialism may be about equality, but of what kind and how much? If there is not a single socialist value but several, as seems likely (for example liberty and equality, individuality and community), what if there is tension between these several values and how are such tensions to be resolved?

In face of all this, it is scarcely surprising that a sample of socialist definitions ranges from the prosaic and institutional (public control of the means of production) to the most audacious and humanistic (free creative development of every individual). Of course, as the most audacious version of socialism, Marxism closes this gap effortlessly through a materialist method whereby the change in the mode of production effected by the victory of the proletariat is also the realization of the humanistic prospectus of unalienated creativity. Yet this remains only one version of socialism, despite its philosophical sweep and the traditional tendency of its adherents to regard it as a comprehensive system that has, so to speak, all the answers. The questions remain, and other socialisms have contributed their own answers. Is socialism to be seen as the victory of a class or the triumph of an idea? Is it the fulfilment of a more general political and intellectual tradition or a rupture from that wider tradition? Is it a science or a morality? Is it revolutionary or evolutionary, centralist or libertarian? These and other questions have provided the material for different socialist traditions, and for a variety of socialist arguments.

In looking at some of these arguments, the earlier definitions suggest a possible starting-point. They indicate that socialists are interested in the promotion of certain social objectives (such as equality and community); and also that they regard the control of the means of production as of central importance as far as such objectives are concerned. The common starting-point for these positions, which has also been the point of departure and divergence, is the socialist critique of the social and economic order spawned by capitalism. This order is variously referred to as the market society, bourgeois society, liberalism, or individualism. Whatever the term used, it describes a society in which self-interest-pursuing, contracting, competing individuals stand as the basic units, traditional social ties are dissolved, the autonomy of economic life from ethical constraints is established, and there are no general social objectives apart from those deriving from the rational pursuit of self-interest. The authentic note of individualism was expressed by Dickens in *Hard Times*:

It was a fundamental principle of the Gradgrind philosophy that everything was to be paid for. Nobody was ever on any account to give anybody anything, or render anybody help without purchase. Gratitude was to be abolished, and the virtues springing from it were not to be. Every inch of the existence of mankind, from birth to death, was to be a bargain across a counter. And if we didn't get to Heaven that way, it was not a politico-economical place, and we had no business there.

It is against such individualism that socialists have mounted their indictment. Indeed, 'socialism' as a view of human sociality is advanced in opposition to that of competitive individualism. The political economy of individualism is attacked for its production of wealth for the few and misery for the many. Thus the indictment of individualism carries with it the two basic socialist positions: the concern with certain values, and the claim that such values are negated because of the appropriation of the means of production by a class. So socialist arguments are hammered out of the assault on capitalism and its philosophy of individualism. The contrast between the new socialism and the old individualism was set out interestingly by Sidney Webb in his *Socialism in England* (1890) in the following table:

INDIVIDUALIST RADICALISM 1840–1874	SOCIALIST RADICALISM 1889
'That the best government is that which governs least.'	'That the best government is that which can safely and successfully administer most.'
Corollary. — Wherever you can make a 'soft place' for a contractor, do so.	*Corollary.* — Wherever the collective organisation of the community can dispense with a contractor or other 'entrepreneur' it should do so.
'That the utmost possible scope should be allowed to individual enterprise in industry.'	'That, wherever possible, industries of widespread public service should be organised and controlled for the public benefit.'
Corollary. — The best social use to which you can turn a profitable monopoly is to hand it over to some lucky individual to make a fortune out of it.	*Corollary.* — Every industry yielding more than a fair remuneration to the actual managers should be 'municipalized' or 'nationalized', or else specially taxed.

'That open competition and complete freedom from legal restrictions furnish the best guarantees of a healthy industrial community.'

Corollary. — John Bright's opinion that adulteration is only a form of competition: the 'individualism' of Mr. Auberon Herbert.

'That only by gradually increasing legal restrictions can the worst competitors be prevented from ousting their better rivals'.

Corollary. — 'The answer of modern statesmanship is that unfettered individual competition is not a principle to which the regulation of industry may be entrusted.' (Mr. John Morley, 'Life of Cobden', Vol. 1., ch. xiii., 298.)

'That the desired end of "equality of opportunity" can be ultimately reached by allowing to each person the complete ownership of any riches he may become possessed of.'

Corollary. — The policy of the 'Liberty and Property Defence League'.

'That Political Economy indubitably proves "equality of opportunity" to be absolutely impossible of even approximate attainment, so long as complete private ownership exists in land and other economic monopolies.'

Corollary. — The policy of 'Nationalization' or 'Municipalization' of Land and other economic monopolies.

'That the best possible social state will result from each individual pursuing his own interest in the way he thinks best.'

Corollary. — 'Private vices, public benefits'.

'That social health is something apart from and above the interest of individuals, and must be consciously pursued as an end in itself.'

Corollary. — The study of the science of sociology, and of the art of politics.

It is the assault on individualism, the ideology of capitalism, that has been the common ground of socialist arguments. This ideological veneer concealed the character of capitalist exploitation. Its competitive, self-regarding values thwarted human co-operation and fraternity. It stunted the individual personality and destroyed the possibility of real community. It elevated private greed and ignored public need. The terms of this indictment are common to the whole range of socialist literature, though the presentation may vary. It at least establishes socialism as what it is not, and what it is against. It is non-capitalism and anti-individualism. Yet this remains a negative identification, and conceals the extent to which from this common basis socialist arguments have taken different, and often conflicting, forms. Socialists may all be against capitalism, but not necessarily on the same grounds; and they may all be in favour of socialism, but again for different reasons and understanding it in different ways.

This may be so at a quite basic level. For example, it has clearly been the case that some socialists, in attacking capitalism, have really been attacking the modernization process itself; while others have been enthusiastic modernizers and have attacked capitalism because of its inefficiency in this respect. Thus socialists like Fourier could attack the new capitalist 'civilization' for its atomism and corruption of natural passions and seek to restore a more organic community, while others, like Saint-Simon, could be excited by the prospect of the new 'industrialism' and seek to realize its potential by releasing it from its individualist constraints. In attacking capitalism, socialists have looked both backwards and forwards, to a lost past and to a new future. This suggests a wider ambiguity within socialism in relation to the age it confronted.

On the one hand, socialism was the creature of the Enlightenment, an expression of the spirit of the age. On the other hand, it stood against the age, and carried a Romantic protest against the new society. This ambiguity is evident with Marx, whose early (and continuing) conception of unalienated, 'whole' man stands alongside a conception of a ruthless process of modernization at the hands of a capitalism destined to create the conditions for socialism. The fact that socialism was seen as the condition for creative, unalienated man may be thought to resolve this ambiguity, or it may be thought instead to make it stand out in sharp relief. What can be said is that much of the early argument between Marx, Proudhon, and Bakunin was grounded in their different orientations to the age they confronted, and their arguments have continued to give different directions to socialist thought. Nor should it be thought that such questions have been resolved: socialists continue to resist the 'logic' of modernity on one side, while on another side they have emerged as its leading agents, in unexpected places.

This problem of the status of socialism has been particularly apparent in its relations with liberalism. Was liberalism to be rejected as the ideological creature of capitalism (as the indictment of 'individualism' suggested), or was the liberal tradition of the Enlightenment to be incorporated into and fulfilled by socialism? Behind this question there lay another: did socialism mark a rupture from existing society, or its further development? Socialism's negative consensus, its assault on capitalist individualism, could serve to prevent any direct engagement with these questions. It was enough to expose the ideological character of liberalism and the classbound nature of its general claims. When socialists used the language of 'wage-slavery' they intended to confront liberalism with the hollowness of its most celebrated emancipatory achievement. Yet this did not resolve the ambiguity surrounding socialism's own relationship to the dominant liberal tradition. On one view socialism stood apart from the entire edifice of bourgeois society, in its own separate and self-contained proletarian culture, equipped with its own proletarian science, a preparation for the time when the bourgeois order would be overthrown and the new society established. Instead of continuity, there was comprehensive opposition, and comprehensive rupture and transcendence.

On another view, however, the task of socialism was to extend and fulfil the prospectus of liberalism, by converting its claims from class into universal terms. If the former view provided the basis for revolutionary communism, the latter became central to the modern social democratic tradition. This tradition acknowledged that it was part of the same cultural universe as liberalism, and in challenging liberalism claimed to be extending it in ways that fulfilled its emancipatory mission. Thus it was claimed that liberty had to be nourished by equality if it was to be universalized, and that this involved extending its scope from the civil and political sphere into the social and economic. 'There is actually no really liberal conception that does not also belong to the elements of the ideas of socialism', wrote Bernstein; while Jaurès announced that 'only socialism will give the Declaration of the Rights of Man its entire meaning'. On this view a socialist was a liberal who really meant it, just as (in the words of a German socialist in 1868) 'democracy must become social democracy if it honestly wants to be democracy'.

The ambiguity about liberalism has been reflected in the range of socialist argument, and has had a considerable impact on socialist politics. This is particularly the case as socialism has shifted its centre of gravity from western Europe, and therefore also away from the liberal inheritance itself. It could no longer be assumed that socialism would build upon the cultural foundations of liberalism, or that socialism would be essentially free and democratic. This was the assumption of the Second International Marxists, but such essentialism could not be sustained after the Bolshevik revolution, when it became necessary either to repudiate the liberal tradition or to affirm socialism's connection with it. The experience of fascism made matters even more pressing, as socialists had to confront the question of whether to make common cause with 'bourgeois' democracy in the face of something worse. What these experiences did reveal was the range of tensions within the general socialist position, tensions that were to sustain divergent socialist traditions.

To put this in another way, it is clear that the socialist argument has been put in a variety of terms, and that some at least of these represent different kinds of socialism. For example, a libertarian socialism has always confronted an organizational socialism. The former has depicted the release of individuality consequent upon the eradication of the oppressive structures of class and state, and has often thought in terms of the self-direction of small communities. It deploys the language of freedom and spontaneity to describe its purpose. By contrast, organizational socialism focuses less upon the unfreedom of capitalism than upon its disorder. It seeks to replace the chaos of capitalist competition, wasteful and undirected as it is, with socialist planning and efficiency. The work of Saint-Simon provides the early source for this type of socialism, with its insistence that the new industrial society requires a new system of organization capable of rational planning. In particular, this involves the replacement of 'politics' by forms of 'administration' run by the key producer groups, 'so as to form a general system of organization directed towards a great common industrial goal'.

Yet here was an advocacy of planning as scientific rationality that was not also statist and centralist. Indeed, it explicitly rejected political centralism in favour of forms of producer self-management as the appropriate organizational model (thereby enabling Durkheim to make his celebrated appropriation of Saint-Simon for his own version of worker socialism, and more generally to attach anarchism to socialism through the connecting thread of producer democracy). In general, though, organizational socialism has embraced the state and central planning as its instruments, and has resisted those socialist currents advocating decentralization and producer control. This has been as true of such reformist traditions as Fabianism, with its collectivism that sought 'to gather the whole people into the State' as Shaw put it, as it has been true of the communist regimes in eastern Europe. This is why the advocates of a libertarian, self-managing socialism have for so long had to operate outside the definitions of socialism offered by both the mainstream social democratic and the mainstream communist traditions.

Socialism as rationality has sustained much socialist argument. Capitalism is indicted less for its injustice and exploitation than for its sheer irrationality as a means of organizing economic life. Indeed, the injustices of capitalism, its production of wealth for the few and misery for the many, have been presented as a consequence of its inability to arrange economic and social life in a rational manner. Thus H. G. Wells (in his *New Worlds for Old*) described how the socialist

wants a complete organisation for all those human affairs that are of collective importance. He says, to take instances almost haphazard, that our ways of manufacturing a great multitude of necessary things, of getting and distributing food, of conducting all sorts of business, of begetting and rearing children, of permitting diseases to engender and spread are chaotic and undisciplined, so badly done that here is enormous hardship, and there enormous waste, here excess and degeneration, and there privation and death. He declares that for these collective purposes, in the satisfaction of these universal needs, mankind presents the appearance and follows the methods of a mob when it ought to follow the method of an army. In place of disorderly individual effort, each man doing what he pleases, the Socialist wants organised effort and a plan.

On this view, then, socialism is not the victory of an exploited class but the triumph of reason. Competition is wasteful and chaotic, and prevents society from solving its collective problems.

This has been a major socialist argument. It places socialism squarely in the Enlightenment tradition and presents it as the most plausible contemporary carrier of this tradition. It presents socialism not as the project of a class but as the general project of a rational humanity. This has given socialism an appeal for members of those groups (intellectuals, scientists, etc.) who are, as it were, professionally interested in this project. It also helps to explain, for example, the wide appeal of Soviet planning in the 1930s when compared with the consequences of capitalist competition elsewhere. The fact that the Soviet Union 'had no unemployment' could make it seem a beacon of socialist rationality in an irrational world, an example of what would be possible if capitalist competition was replaced by socialist planning. However, it also illustrated the tendency for socialist rationality to turn into an enforced rule of reason, whether by a Leninist party endowed with superior consciousness or Beatrice Webb's 'élite of unassuming experts' (the fact that the Webbs fell in love with the Soviet Union should be seen less as personal idiosyncrasy and more as an example of the affinities generated by a socialism of social discipline and rational order). Socialist rationality required its guardians, just as it required the suppression of 'irrational' elements.

Of course, socialism may be seen as *both* a class project *and* the general project of a rational humanity. Instead of the establishment of a system of socialism-as-rationalism being regarded as the remedy for the ills suffered by an exploited class, the victory of that class could be seen as the remedy for the ills suffered by humanity as a whole. The belief that this is so leads easily to the view that nothing is more important than the victory of this class, to which all else should be subordinated, since the future of humanity itself depends upon it. Most socialists have framed their arguments in terms of class categories, at least in the sense in which they have depicted capitalism as a system of class exploitation and socialism as the means whereby such exploitation would be ended; but they have differed on the extent to which socialism is *exclusively* a matter of class analysis and class action. If socialism is about classes, is it not also about individuals? If it is about class power, is it not also about social justice? If it is about class exploitation, is it not also about other forms of exploitation? If it is the movement of a class, is it not also a general movement of people?

Such questions serve to mark out different socialist positions. Marxism has provided the basis for one set of answers, with its emphasis on the centrality of the mode of production and its class character as giving society its decisive shape. Marx's celebrated formulation of this position in the 1859 Preface to *A Critique of Political Economy* provides a marker:

In the social production of their life, men enter into definite relations that are indispensable and independent of their will, relations of production which correspond to a definite stage of development of their material productive forces. The sum total of these relations of production constitutes the economic structure of society, the real foundation, on which rises a legal and political superstructure and to which correspond definite forms of social consciousness. The mode of production of material life conditions the social, political, and intellectual life process in general. It is not the consciousness of men that determines their being, but, on the contrary, their social being that determines their consciousness.

The terms of this formulation have provided the material for much socialist argument, and continuing dispute.

Some of this argument has been of the 'what Marx really meant' kind, with much dancing on the terms 'condition' and 'determine' in a bid to hammer out the extent to which Marx was, or was not, a determinist and the purveyor of social laws. Certainly many Marxists have read him in this way, but that may not be altogether Marx's fault. Similarly, other socialists have rejected what they have taken to be Marx's determinism even when they have accepted his general account of the centrality of the mode of production. Traditionally, Marxists have adopted a rigid attachment to the base–superstructure model of society as the universal tool of social analysis, whereas there have been other socialists who have wanted to assert at least a partially independent role for elements of the 'superstructure' (such as politics and the state) and to operate within this space for socialist purposes. What Marx's formulation does reveal, however, is the essentially class character of his analysis and the repudiation of other approaches, including those of other socialists. Marx's units are classes not individuals, for individuals only have social significance in terms of class membership and they are in every sense socially determined beings. For Marxism this raised questions about the generation of socialist consciousness and the process of social change, but for other socialists it represented an unacceptable devaluation of what it meant to be an individual human being.

This basic difference was reflected in other implications of Marx's production theory of society. It carried with it a rejection of any view of socialism that involved the framing of desired ends or values and then the construction of means towards their realization. Such an approach simply did not make sense in terms of a production theory of social determination. It was utopian, idealistic, unscientific. Similarly, Marx's productionism was at odds with those versions of socialist distributionism that sought to reallocate social goods in terms of such notions as 'equality' or 'justice', for this was an individualist approach of claims and rewards that obscured the real determinant of social allocation, namely the class character of the mode of production. Thus Karl Kautsky explained how an early socialism that had been preoccupied with principles of distribution had been superseded by a socialism that realized that 'the distribution of products in a community is determined . . . by the prevailing system of production'. Some socialists, and most of the critics of socialism, might persist in treating socialism as a theory of distribution, but it was essentially a theory of production. This enabled Stalin to dismiss the idea of equality of consumption as 'a reactionary petty-bourgeois absurdity worthy of some primitive sect of ascetics'.

Such a dismissal carried all the weight of scientific socialism behind it. It serves as a reminder of the extent to which socialism has presented a scientific doctrinal face to the world—although this has not been its only face. Socialism as social morality has coexisted, not always easily, with socialism as social science. The Marxian distinction between socialism 'scientific' and socialism 'utopian' was designed to bury the latter, a burial that has been widely accepted; notwithstanding the fact that a 'utopian' like Saint-Simon claimed to be essentially a social scientist while the 'scientific' Marx, at least on one view, looks like the supreme utopian. The scientific socialists have presented socialism as the science of society, able to explain the determinants of social structure and the motor of social change. They have seen socialism as *essentially* scientific, equipped with a historical science that identifies the determining role of the mode of production in historical change, a social science that identifies the class basis of contemporary society, and an economic science that identifies the process of capitalist exploitation. The scientific socialist claims to be in possession of a comprehensive and self-contained method of social analysis that has yielded a body of truths. Both the method and the truths are defended resolutely, because they constitute the status of socialism. It has been left to other socialists to distinguish the scientifically true from the ethically desirable, and to give some attention to the latter.

The scientifically true also has a habit of becoming the historically inevitable. Much socialist argument has been sustained by a comforting sense that history is on its side. This is as true of the reformist Fabians who pointed to the relentless, historical march of collectivism as it is of the revolutionary Marxists who confidently awaited that historical moment when capitalism would finally collapse and the proletariat would inaugurate socialism. In *Capital* Marx described the process that would usher in the great historical climax:

Along with the constantly diminishing number of the magnates of capital, who usurp and monopolise all the advantages of this process of transformation, grows the mass of misery, oppression, slavery, degradation, exploitation; but with this too grows the revolt of the working class, a class ever increasing in numbers and disciplined, united, organised by the very mechanism of capitalist production itself. The monopoly of capital becomes a fetter upon the mode of production, which has sprung up and flourished along with it and under it. Centralisation of the means of production and socialisation of labour at last reach a point where they become incompatible with their capitalist integument. This integument is burst asunder. The knell of capitalist private property sounds. The expropriators are expropriated.

Here is a historical drama the script of which is already written, and with the proletariat required to act out its necessary role at the appropriate historical moment. It produces the familiar picture of socialists waiting for capitalism's final, decisive crisis, when the proletariat will fulfil its historical task. It has been a long wait.

Not all socialist argument has been of this kind, of course. Some socialists have denied that there is anything historically necessary about socialism, for there could be other successors to capitalism even if capitalism was to collapse. Similarly, the working class could well fail to act in the way scripted for it. Even if socialism was historically necessary, this by itself did not make it desirable. So some socialists rejected history in favour of action, whether the sort of insurrectionary action that cut across any nice judgement about historical ripeness or the balance of forces, or the gentler sort of action that involved the pursuit of a freely chosen ideal. When R. H. Tawney urged people to 'choose equality' it was an invitation to make history not to respond to its imperatives.

Among socialists who have taken values seriously, there has been wide agreement that equality should be regarded as a key socialist value, perhaps even *the* socialist value. Socialism has addressed itself to the structure of society, and sought to replace the unequal social structure of market capitalism with a structure of equality. At bottom, this involves a moral commitment to equality as a value, for it would not be enough to expose existing inequalities without also mounting a case for equality itself (and in moral terms that withstand defences of inequality on the assorted grounds of liberty, enterprise, welfare, etc.). Thus socialists, from a variety of perspectives, have anchored their commitment to equality in a view of the equal worth of all individuals, and have presented their egalitarian proposals as extensions and applications of this basic position. Tawney's *Equality* remains perhaps the most powerful and sustained argument of this kind, but even this also serves as a reminder that there are difficulties in concluding that socialism is essentially about equality (as was argued, for example, by Crosland in his *The Future of Socialism*). Partly this is because socialists have disagreed about what is involved in a commitment to equality, stretching from the sort of militant egalitarianism that makes equality its single, absolute value ('Let there be no other difference between people than that of age or sex', in the words of Babeuf's *Manifesto of the Equals*), to the moderate egalitarianism that distinguishes equality of treatment from identity of treatment and addresses itself to the elimination of unjustifiable inequalities.

However, this is not the only difficulty involved in enthroning equality as socialism's sovereign value. There is the further difficulty that socialism espouses not one value but several, and socialist positions are forged out of this cluster of values. For example, socialists have embraced equality but they have also

embraced liberty, unwilling to allow the latter to be appropriated
by individualism. Some socialists have invented a 'socialist' liberty that has nothing to do with its 'bourgeois' version (just as
they have invented a socialist 'democracy' that has nothing to do
with bourgeois parliamentarianism), but other socialists have
wanted to be both equal and free and have advanced an argument
for equality that is not only sensitive to the claims of liberty but
seeks to extend and strengthen it. Indeed, in some socialist arguments equality is advanced *for* liberty, as the means whereby the
positive freedoms of activity and choice are enlarged for most
people. 'The aim of socialism', declared Clement Attlee, 'is to
give greater freedom to the individual.' This is not the only sense
in which equality begins to look like an instrumental socialist
value, the servant of other values, in socialist arguments. What
seems to be a case for equality as the central socialist value frequently turns out on closer inspection (as with Tawney) to be a
case for the role of equality in promoting such values as fraternity, fellowship, and community; and it is these that are consid-
ered fundamental.

This suggests a further point about the nature and extent of
socialism's ultimate claims. These have ranged from the prosaic
to the transcendental. Socialism has stood for welfare and security, claiming to end the miseries of poverty and unemployment
caused by capitalism. If it is objected that this is not 'socialism',
the answer is that many socialists have believed that this is precisely what socialism involves. Other socialists have gone beyond
this welfare objective to suggest that socialism has wider consequences for social life, producing, for example, a greater 'seren-
ity', as Aneurin Bevan once described it, or a growth of co-operation, community, and fraternity. Yet this does not exhaust the
range of socialism's claims. It has been possible to envisage, as
with Owen, a transformation in human nature consequent upon
a change in its environment. Most ambitious of all, as with Marx,
socialism has been presented as nothing less than a prospectus for
rehumanization, the recovery of human unity and subjectivity
consequent upon the abolition of socially determined human
alienation. In this 'dream of perfect unity' as Kolakowski
describes it, there is a fusion of political and civil society, of
collective man and individual man, of social life and private life.
It is one of the many ironies in socialism's history that such a

fusion has indeed been achieved, and in the name of Marx, but scarcely in a form that Marx would recognize as the emancipatory realm of self-determining creativity. Whether the dream has nourished the nightmare is another matter.

What emerges from all this is that there is no single socialist argument, just as there is no single socialist tradition. Moreover, there is not merely a plurality of socialist arguments, but tension, ambiguity, and even conflict between them. The following table attempts to indicate, in shorthand, some of the forms that the socialist argument has taken:

Doctrine	Values
History	Action
Determinism	Voluntarism
Revolution	Reform
Production	Distribution
Rationalism	Moralism
Centralism	Decentralism
Class	Individual
Equality	Liberty
State	Community
Modernization	Restoration
Welfare	Wholeness
Order	Self-management
Bureaucracy	Democracy

It should be emphasized that this list is intended simply to illustrate some of the terrain and tensions of socialist arguments. It is not exhaustive, and other terms could have been employed at almost every point. Nor are the couplings intended to denote opposites, for often it is a matter of emphasis or approach. Moreover, actual socialist positions can and do accommodate different approaches, for example doctrine *and* values, rationalism *and* moralism, equality *and* liberty. Yet the differences are important, and have sustained different socialist traditions. Scientific, doctrinal socialism has taken its stand on different ground from ethical socialism. A socialism that is immanent in history is not the same as a socialism that attaches itself to human energy and will. A socialism that builds down from the state differs from one that builds up from the community. An organizational socialism of order, planning, and bureaucracy rubs up against a libertarian socialism of direct democracy and self-management. A reformist socialism of improvement and persuasion has a different basis from a revolutionary socialism of rupture and transcendence. A socialism that promises more security, more equality, more freedom, or simply more 'decency', to use Orwell's term, has different ambitions from a socialism that promises a total transformation of every aspect of human existence—and so on.

Such tensions do not themselves constitute distinct socialist traditions, but they indicate the sort of terrain on which different kinds of socialism have developed. In practice, of course, socialist arguments take different forms in different places, as well as in the same place over time. New evidence and experience extends the range of argument or changes its focus. Thus the experience of 'actually existing socialism' demands a response from a doctrinal socialism that maintains a particular position in relation to the determining character of the mode of production. Likewise, feminism raises questions for a socialism that fixes its eyes on the exploitation of class in the waged economy, but has a blind spot for the exploitation of gender in the domestic economy. As arguments develop and are restated, so socialist theories are reassessed (as in the endless reincarnation of Marx as economic determinist or revolutionary humanist). Socialist positions are constructed out of real and inescapable tensions (for example, between state and community, economic planning and producer freedom, egalitarianism and diversity), unless it is believed that no such tensions exist and that there is only one kind of socialism. At the end of the twentieth century this is a difficult belief to sustain. Moreover, the great Marxian 'synthesis' that once claimed to resolve all socialism's internal tensions has long since fallen apart under their strain.

Most of what follows is concerned to illustrate the variety of socialism by looking more closely at what are taken to be some of its central questions and tensions. Is its method that of reform or revolution? What is the structural form of socialism? Who are the actors who are to bring socialism about?

3. Doctrines

Put in the simplest and most basic terms, socialism has
both an empirical theory and a moral doctrine.

Bernard Crick

Beneath the variety of socialist arguments, about ends and
means, strategies and actors, there lurks a more basic distinction
affecting the form that these arguments have taken. Indeed, it is a
distinction that defines the status of socialism, in the sense that it
indicates the essential foundations upon which socialist arguments are constructed. The distinction was glimpsed in the tensions discussed earlier, between science and values, rationalism
and moralism. Socialism has presented itself as two kinds of
doctrine, a positive doctrine of analysis and explanation and a
normative one of morality and values.

To identify this distinction, and to insist on its importance, is
not to suggest that actual socialisms can be neatly distinguished in
terms of their different kinds of doctrinal basis. In practice,
socialists have tended to be both rationalists and moralists,
combining theoretical analysis with moral valuation. The two
lines of doctrinal argument have been reinforcive, each calling in
the aid of the other to extend the argument and strengthen the
position. For example, early British socialism was founded upon
both the theoretical account of exploitation provided by the so-
called Ricardian socialists with their labour theory of value *and*
the Owenite moral indictment of market capitalism. This dualism
continued to sustain British socialism later, as a Fabian rationalism with its theory of economic 'rent', which extended an analysis of exploitation to include the capitalist as well as the landlord
(designed to trump both liberalism and Marxism), and doctrine
of collectivism was combined with the sort of moral arguments
mounted by the ethical socialists associated with the Independent
Labour Party. Moreover, if socialist moralists have readily aug-
mented their critique of capitalism and advocacy of socialism
with the armoury supplied by a socialist rationalism, even the

most severely rationalist of socialists have often revealed, when lightly scratched, a soft underbelly of moralism.

Indeed, the metaphor of soft underbelly is less appropriate than that of tough inner skin. This is clearly the case with Marx, for the reader of *Capital* soon discovers that the analysis of capitalist exploitation is a matter not merely of political economy but of moral passion. More generally, Marx's values, most prominent in the early, 'humanist' Marx but remaining central to his mature position, shape the view of socialist man that in turn sustains the whole socialist project. They are robustly republican values, and point towards the recovery of human subjectivity beyond capitalism. As Kolakowski puts it: 'the notion that Marx regarded socialism as a system for depressing individuals into a Comtean universal being deprived of all subjectivity is one of the absurdest aberrations to which the study of his work has given rise.' Even the dry old Fabians, with their elaborate exercises in historical sociology designed to establish the pedigree of collectivism, turn out on closer inspection to be rationalists in search of the conditions for moral unity and consensus in society.

So rationalists are moralists, and moralists are rationalists, whether they look like it or admit to it. This merely testifies to the fact that socialism is a doctrine in both the senses identified here, and necessarily so. It is a philosophical account of the moral superiority of socialism to capitalism, but it is also a theoretical account of how societies are actually structured and the determinants of this structure. This necessary dualism may seem to devalue the significance of the distinction that forms its basis, yet this is not so when viewed against the historical development of socialism itself. In this light the distinction between the two kinds of doctrine takes on a considerable significance, because it has been regarded as significant by socialists themselves who have sought to construct socialist positions on the basis of it. Doctrine as theory has not gone hand in hand with doctrine as values, even if they are necessary and natural partners and even though their coexistence may be detected where it is not normally expected or where it is formally denied. Some socialists seem to have contented themselves with a sort of moralistic whistling in the wind, a comforting stance that could prove disabling (as Ramsay MacDonald, for example, discovered) when hands have to be dirtied in the engagement with capitalism. Other socialists have repudiated the language of values and wrapped themselves in a 'scientific' doctrine that has all the answers, a stance occasioning its own trail of disabilities in the face of a historical process that, perversely, goes on asking new questions.

When Marx opened fire on the utopians he described his target as 'doctrinaire socialism'. By this he meant systems of society that are the mental inventions of particular thinkers (*'petty bourgeois'*), utopian constructions that correspond to the undeveloped state of the class struggle. He wrote the following in his *Poverty of Philosophy*:

So long as the proletariat is not yet sufficiently developed to constitute itself as a class, these theoreticians are merely utopians who, to meet the wants of the oppressed classes, improvise systems and go in search of a regenerating science. But in the measure that history moves forward, and with it the struggle of the proletariat assumes clearer outlines, they no longer need to seek science in their minds; they have only to take note of what is happening before their eyes and become its mouthpiece . . . From this moment, science, which is a product of the historical movement, has associated with it, has ceased to be doctrinaire, and has become revolutionary.

So here is the distinction between a doctrinaire (utopian) science and a revolutionary science, with the elevation of the latter and devaluation of the former. One is ultimately baseless (and becomes reactionary), while the other is securely rooted in the historical process itself and represents the viewpoint of the class that is the progressive agent in that process. Thus socialists like Proudhon are to be denounced because they do not understand this process and invent unavailable and historically regressive social orders, while indulging in a merely moralistic criticism of the competitive system.

Here, then, is the repudiation of one version of 'doctrinaire' socialism and the development of another. The object of attack is a false and undeveloped conception of what constitutes a scientific approach, as well as the appeal to morals in socialist argument. It should be repeated that the 'utopian' socialists made extravagant claims to scientific status, as evidenced by Saint-Simon's belief that he was the founder of the new science of industrial society. It should also be recalled that the nineteenth century was the period when the Enlightenment tradition prompted social thinkers of all persuasions, influenced by the prestige of the natural sciences, to set about constructing a science of society. The historical development of societies came to be widely regarded as a patterned process, and assorted attempts were made to translate these patterns into social laws that pointed forwards as well as backwards in their explanatory ambitions. These considerations are relevant to any understanding of the sense in which Marx has come to be regarded as the founder of 'scientific socialism'.

This is difficult and still contentious ground, but a number of points need to be made for present purposes. For example, it is necessary to register some distinction between Marx and the 'scientific' Marxism constructed out of his legacy. It seems fairly clear that he was not in the business of imitating the physical sciences, even though he was not unwilling to trade off some of the favourable associations to which such imitation gave rise. As already seen, his own 'science' claimed to be rooted in the observable reality of historical development and social movements, unlike the 'fantastic' science of the utopian socialists. It was a claim to be engaged in empirical theory, in the sense in which Lichtheim says that 'it was only after Marx had intervened that socialists began to understand how capitalism actually worked'. It was not a claim therefore to have discovered the 'iron laws' of history, as frequently alleged. Indeed, late in life Marx ridiculed the notion of 'using as one's master key a general historico-philosophical theory, the supreme virtue of which consists in being super-historical'. Instead, Marx's production theory of society was to be seen (as he said) as a 'guiding thread' that indicated general conditioning factors, not as laws of iron determination. Thus modern interpreters of Marx's work are able to present his social theory as essentially a 'research hypothesis' (the phrase belongs to Terrell Carver, one such interpreter).

However, when all this is duly registered, something more still needs to be said. If Marx's general social theory, with its focus on the central role of technology and the mode of production, can be treated in this way, the same is not true of his narrower economic theory, with its account of value and surplus value and of the dynamics of capitalism's contradictions, crises, and collapse. In no sense does this have the character of a research hypothesis, but carries the certainty of verifiable causal analysis. Moreover, it is this Marx, the mature economist and scientific analyst of capitalism, who was to provide the basis for a subsequent, comprehensive 'scientific socialism', armed with economic laws. Furthermore, even if Marx's social theory is presented in terms of the identification of tendencies rather than a system of rigid determination, the fact remains that it was regarded by its author as a system. It was all-embracing and self-sufficient; it did not require the advance of knowledge in the social and human sciences or contributions from other disciplines; and while there might be other socialist doctrines there was only one that had scientific status and social significance.

So here was a doctrinaire socialism, partly in the necessary sense of open, empirical theory, but also in the closed sense attaching to a particular view of what constitutes a science. Two further features can be noted at this point. First, Marx's doctrine claimed to combine analysis and action, theory and practice, understanding the world and changing it. This involved, crucially, the identification of an agency through which such a combination would be effected, and through which the historical process would work itself out. For Marx, of course, this agency was the proletariat, but the discovery of this agency looks more like a philosophical act on Marx's part than an empirical one. In the formulation to be found in *The Holy Family*: 'It is not a question of what this or that proletarian, or even the whole proletariat, at the moment *regards* as its aim. It is a question of *what the proletariat is*, and what, in accordance with this *being*, it will historically be compelled to do. Its aim and historical action is visibly and irrevocably foreshadowed in its own life situation as well as in the whole organisation of bourgeois society today.' If Marx can be at least partially acquitted of some of the wilder charges of historicism and scientism of the kind levelled by many of his traditional critics, it remains the case that his position represents more than a 'method' or set of analytical tools, as suggested by some contemporary Marxists. It extends into a doctrine about the direction and agency of historical development that encompasses the future as well as the past and culminates in a communism that is presented as nothing less than the end of 'prehistory'.

Secondly, in terms of the kinds of socialist doctrine identified here, Marx's position represents the most unequivocal and fundamental repudiation of socialism as moral doctrine. To repeat the point, this has nothing to do with the question of whether Marx himself was animated by values, a question to which an affirmative answer has already been given. What is central here is Marx's assertion that the indictment of capitalism has to be grounded in historical and economic analysis and not in any independent moral argument. Indeed, any such belief in an independent moral arena is fundamentally misconceived, since it fails to recognize the dependence of moral positions and the terms of the moral vocabulary upon material interests.

Ethical considerations are irrelevant to the analysis of capitalism, as irrelevant as the attribution of moral responsibility to individual capitalists or the belief that individuals have a social and moral significance apart from their class position. As Marx explained in the preface to *Capital*:

Individuals are dealt with only in so far as they are the personification of economic categories, embodiments of particular class relations and class interests. My standpoint, from which the evolution of the economic formation of society is viewed as a process of natural history, can less than any other make the individual responsible for relations whose creature he socially remains.

Further, it is equally misconceived to think in terms of the working class defining the values that would constitute their emancipation and then setting about the task of realizing them through action. There could be no separation of this kind, for it is only through the activity of emancipation in the historical process that the aims actually being pursued come to be understood. There can thus be no distinction between fact and value, between what is and what ought to be; nor between freedom and necessity. It is clear from this that not merely is Marx unable to provide socialism with an ethical basis or moral philosophy, but his formulation of the socialist project denies the need for any such provision to be undertaken.

These brief remarks are intended to get the character and status of Marx's doctrine into some sort of focus. This is necessary in order to navigate the crossing between Marx and Marxism in the latter part of the nineteenth century, a crucial period when Marxism not only consolidated its ascendancy over other versions of socialism, but also asserted its credentials as a comprehensive science of society. No longer was it to be presented, if it ever had been, as dealing in research hypotheses and methods of empirical enquiry, but as a rigid doctrine of economic laws and historical determination. Here was a fully fledged scientific socialism, a term proudly displayed and impressive in its range and scope. The consecration of Marx's work as scientific socialism was a development of considerable significance for the general history of socialism, as both movement and doctrine. It was a development that occurred firstly during the period of the Second International in the generation before 1914, then secondly and more durably when Marxism became the official ideology of the Soviet regime. Thus in fact two developments, both relevant to the discussion here, took place. The ascendancy of Marxism over other kinds of socialism represented the ascendancy of one understanding of socialist doctrine. Utopian and moralistic traditions were marginalized from the socialist mainstream, diverted into anarchism and syndicalism, or lay in wait to provide the foundation for later revisionist and reformist tendencies. The further development was the extension of Marx's work into a body of scientific socialist doctrine that served for an important period as the integrating ideology of international socialism. During this period socialism assumed for itself the status of a comprehensive scientific doctrine, not a moral doctrine or modest empirical theory, and presented itself to the world—and the world to itself—in those terms.

This is not the place to explore the process whereby this development took place. The role of Engels, who tends to get a bad press these days in this respect, is usually identified as central. The words of his famous speech at Marx's graveside set the tone: 'Just as Darwin discovered the law of development of organic nature, so Marx discovered the law of development of human history.' Engels's own work, especially his *Anti-Dühring*, which appeared after Marx's death, came to be accepted as the authoritative frame of reference through which Marx's work was to be viewed. The effect of this was to systematize Marxism into a complete body of scientific knowledge, sustained by a method that was now elevated into a 'dialectical materialism' that was universal in its application, embracing even the natural world itself. Through Engels Marxism was therefore reinforced in its status as a complete and self-contained science of society, and socialism was reinforced in a status independent of moral values because it became rooted in a revealed process of historical determination. In identifying the role of Engels in this systematization of Marxism, it should also be said that he was accurately reflecting a late-nineteenth-century climate of ideas that was saturated with scientism, positivism, and historicism. It would have been difficult to resist such a climate. In Engels's case, attached as he was to the natural sciences, the task was not to resist this climatic penetration of Marxism but to fully assimilate Marxism to it.

This enterprise proved entirely successful and shaped the presentation of the socialist argument for at least a generation (and, in a sense, for much longer). Before looking at some examples of what this involved, it is important to register the general and essential effect of this understanding and presentation of the socialist position. It produced a particular mode of argument, a doctrinaire mode that packaged up socialism into a tight scientific system. In terms of the general development of socialism, there is a real sense in which this mode of argument was more significant than the content of its particular doctrines. In other words, socialists came to believe that they understood the historical process, and that this understanding anchored their political activity in a secure scientific basis. The main elements of this basis are familiar enough (for example, Marx's account of historical stages, the determining role of the mode of production, the fatal contradictions of capitalism, the revolutionary mission of the proletariat), but their combined effect was to enthrone socialism as a complete scientific system, a status that was to be defended against critics and upheld in the face of difficult evidence. A further effect was that any doctrinal developments or innovations (for example, concerning the exact nature of capitalism's collapse, or the analysis of imperialism) had to be presented and claimed as a reinforcement of Marxism's scientific status at points of possible vulnerability, rather than as an erosion of that status in any way.

What this status ensured was the necessary character of the transition from capitalism to socialism. This was, so to speak, the bottom line of scientific socialism. It was an outcome that did not depend upon an act of will or exercises in moral persuasion. Nor was it an outcome that was contingent or merely available. So here was a scientific doctrine that was also a doctrine with political implications in the world of historical action. One important implication was that socialists constantly sought to locate their political activity within the terms of doctrinal orthodoxy, even (or perhaps especially) when such activity seemed to point in contrary directions. Doctrinal orthodoxy guaranteed the success of the activity, or so it was believed, or at least bestowed legitimacy upon it. Something of what this involved in practice will be seen shortly. There is one further general feature of the scientific mode of argument identified here that should be noticed. The belief in doctrinal completeness constantly tempted 'scientific' socialists to reduce and compress evidence into ready-made explanatory categories that left no room for loose ends. This is reflected, as Ralph Miliband has said, in an attitude of mind to which Marxists have been prone: 'This is the belief that because A and B are not *totally* different, they are not *really* different at all.' Yet history has been full of loose ends, and these have posed particular problems for those socialists who believe they have solved its riddles.

This belief was central to pre-1914 socialist orthodoxy in Europe, which is why the events of 1914 produced such a trauma. It was capitalism that was supposed to collapse, not socialist internationalism. Nationalism was supposed to be eclipsed by the forces making for global revolution. The ability of events to inflict such damage on socialist positions (in 1914, and then in 1917) was precisely because socialists had converted Marxism into an allegedly impregnable theoretical system. Thus Karl Kautsky, the Second International's leading theoretician and upholder of doctrinal orthodoxy, had founded Marxism's status upon its historical materialism, which, uniquely, was able to explain how a process of capitalist maturation would usher in the victory of the proletariat and the establishment of socialism. Kautsky hitched Darwinism to Engels's initial codification of Marxism to produce a version of socialism as historical science that unravelled the motor and direction of social development. 'Marxist socialism', he declared, 'is nothing else, in the final analysis, than the science of history with the viewpoint of the proletariat at its point of departure.'

Kautsky is always taken as the symbol of doctrinal orthodoxy in this period, but the more significant point is that his mode of argument, with its emphasis on the essentially scientific character of socialism, was itself a reflection of a prevailing orthodoxy. For example, Rosa Luxemburg, a leading figure on the left wing of German social democracy who maintained a vigorously independent line on a range of questions, was supremely orthodox in her insistence that socialism had to be securely rooted in an analysis that showed it to be objectively necessary. It was this insistence that led her to advance a particular economic analysis (in her theory of accumulation) of the exact conditions and reasons why Marx's general account of capitalist collapse would be vindicated. Her analysis was idiosyncratic in terms of the prevailing Marxist orthodoxy on this matter, but reflected the need to prevent any doubt that socialism could provide a scientific demonstration of the inevitability of capitalism's downfall. More generally, Plekhanov (usually described as the father of Russian Marxism) carried the codification of Marxism still further, expounding and defending its status as a complete philosophical system and presenting it in the form of handbooks or manuals. This was an approach that later characterized the official Marxism that became the state ideology of the Soviet Union. Even where Marx's work was genuinely extended, as it was by the Austro–Marxist Hilferding in his analysis of finance capital and imperialism, to take account of developments in the international economy, its viewpoint and conclusion were still those of an orthodoxy that saw its task as identifying the trends presaging the destruction of capitalism and the victory of the proletariat.

So here was a scientific socialism that exhibited great intellectual distinction in its construction of elaborate theoretical systems demonstrating, with the reasons discovered by Marx, why socialism is immanent in history. If the focus here is on the science and the immanence, at the expense of the constructs themselves, the reason is that these are the defining characteristics of this kind of socialism. Moreover, its adherents have always wanted to affirm that this is so, whatever their particular disagreements. Thus Rosa Luxemburg, in the controversy over Bernstein's revisionism, explained why the theory of capitalist collapse was central to scientific socialism, for 'if one admits, with Bernstein, that capitalist development does not move in the direction of its own ruin, then socialism ceases to be objectively necessary'. In the same context, Kautsky wrote that 'if once the materialistic conception of history and the conception of the proletariat as the motive force of the coming social revolution were abandoned, then I would have to admit that I was through, that my life no longer had any meaning'.

It should also be said that scientific socialism has been able to command a wide appeal and exercise considerable influence precisely on the basis of its allegedly scientific status. This was recognized by the French syndicalist, Sorel, for whom scientific socialism was true in a pragmatic sense, as an ideological weapon to sustain the proletariat in its revolutionary mission. It would be possible to document the way in which individual socialists have been profoundly influenced by the historical certainties offered by scientific socialism. To take just two examples, both British: William Morris described how he was 'in for a fine pessimistic end of life' until his outlook was transformed by the knowledge that 'the seeds of a great change, what we others call Social-Revolution, were beginning to germinate'. Then later John Strachey, the most effective exponent of the communist version of Marxism in the 1930s, described as 'the essential argument in its favour' the fact that it was 'the one method by which human civilisation can be maintained at all'. This line of argument prompted one observer to remark (presciently, in view of Strachey's subsequent renunciation of Marx and embrace of Keynes) that 'one clearly feels that had there been any possibility of preserving the bourgeois system healthy and progressive, Strachey would not have been for changing it'.

If the events of 1914 blew a hole in the immaculate doctrinal structure of Second International socialism, and began the process of formal and final rupture within international socialism, the events of 1917 turned the hole into a chasm. In terms of doctrinal orthodoxy, the Bolshevik revolution should not have happened. Instead of a mature capitalism with a developed working class providing the site for socialism, as described by orthodox scientific socialism, here was a revolutionary seizure of power in a peasant society lacking both the political and the economic development that it was the historic task of capitalism to bring about as the basis for socialism. Hence the opposition to Leninism mounted by both Kautsky and Plekhanov, the accepted guardians of Marxist orthodoxy: the economic conditions were wrong, and the revolution could only be sustained by repression.

However, if this judgement was doctrinally correct, and even if it was vindicated by subsequent developments, it was also a reflection on the vulnerabilities of scientific socialism that it could find itself so exposed and undermined by historical events. The golden age of scientific socialism had come to an end, and its mantle was now appropriated and deployed as the official ideology of Soviet communism, except that its scientific credentials were now rooted in what became known as Marxism–Leninism.

In many respects it is Lenin who provides the most telling epitaph to the ascendancy and decline of doctrinaire socialism. This is not, as is often claimed, because he was the revolutionary opportunist who drove the bulldozer of practice through the cathedral of theory (or, to put it more plainly, because he was a socialist of the deed and not of the book). Rather, it is because he was precisely the opposite, a supremely doctrinaire socialist who always insisted on hammering out his practice on the anvil of theory (as is emphasized and documented in Neil Harding's study of *Lenin's Political Thought*). The task was to root revolutionary practice in a secure theoretical position. Thus, by 1917, Lenin had satisfied himself that socialist revolution in Russia was authorized by his theory of monopoly capitalism and imperialism, that 'the objective process of development is such that it is *impossible* to advance from monopolies (and the war has magnified their number, role and importance ten-fold) without advancing towards socialism'. So Lenin was, in Harding's words, 'an extraordinarily doctrinaire politician', whose practical activity represented the relentless application of theoretical positions even when circumstances seemed wholly unpropitious and when he himself was in a minority. Leninism was the culmination of a Marxist tradition in which theory was endowed with a predictive quality, able to unravel the *future* course of social development and requiring only that socialist practice should synchronize with it. Lenin's victory was, therefore, the consummation of this tradition and not its abrogation. Yet its consummation was also its disintegration, when the theoretical underpinning of Lenin's position (the anticipation of global revolution born out of the havoc wreaked by imperialism) was swept away by the failure of events to behave as theory predicted. Lenin's revolution was rooted in doctrine, not opportunism, but the nature of its success provided a testimony to the disabilities of the whole doctrinal tradition of scientific socialism. The essential point is not, of course, that its theory was wrong, but that it rested upon a fundamental misunderstanding of what theory was and of its role in socialist politics.

Something of this kind was argued by Bernstein, which is why his 'revisionism' was rounded on so ferociously by the orthodox of the Second International. In challenging some of the leading elements of the prevailing Marxist orthodoxy (the theory of value, proletarian impoverishment, class polarization, capitalist collapse) and in suggesting the reformist implications of such revision, he was also challenging the entire schematic, scientific basis of that orthodoxy. In terms of the base–superstructure relationship contained in Marx's production theory, Bernstein argued the need to give 'the ideological, and especially the ethical, factors greater space for independent activity than was formerly the case'. Similarly, if economic forces alone could not be relied upon to deliver socialism, then it was necessary in Bernstein's view to construct a separate moral case for socialism. In other words, one kind of socialist doctrine had to be at least complemented by another. This marked an important moment in the development of the modern social democratic tradition, although this development was already apparent in the political practice, if not in the theoretical utterances, of many of those who denounced revisionism.

It was also apparent in the character of socialist arguments heard outside Germany, the home of Second International orthodoxy. For example, in the case of Jaurès, the leader of French socialism, his adherence to Marxism stopped short at regarding it as a total system and he drew freely upon other traditions. In particular, he presented socialism not merely as a scientific doctrine but as an expression of humanity's long, conscious pursuit of moral values. Beneath the doctrinal umbrella of the Second International, Jaurès and Kautsky represented different kinds of socialism. To Jaurès, socialism was essentially a matter of values; to Kautsky, it was above all else a comprehensive science of society. Then there was British socialism, in which Marxist influence was small and had anyway been countered by a Fabianism that, refusing to feel inferior theoretically to Marxism, claimed to offer in its theory of economic rent an account of capitalist exploitation superior to that of Marx's theory of surplus value, and in its historical analysis an account of the direction of social development (described by Sidney Webb in *Fabian Essays* as 'the irresistible sweep of social tendencies') that provided the basis, at least in England, for a politics of collectivist reform. The first Fabians were not mere empiricists, as is frequently alleged, but doctrinaires (though of the kind that did not demand the enforcement of orthodoxy). However, the central and distinguishing fact about British socialism was that it was imbued with a deep moralism, drawn from a variety of sources. In Tawney's phrase, it was a socialist tradition that was 'unashamedly ethical'. If this isolated it from the world of pre-1914 scientific socialism, when it was relegated to the status of a theoretically primitive poor relation, it later enabled it to play a role in the construction of a democratic socialism upon a different basis.

The mode of socialist argument discussed here, that has elevated theory to the status of scientific doctrine, has carried with it a number of consequences for socialist politics. The example of Lenin has already provided one dramatic illustration of such a consequence, but it is possible to identify a range of others, both particular and general. For example, the sort of determinism that conditioned the outlook of the pre-1914 German Social Democratic Party, with its belief in the maturation of capitalism as the necessary prelude to the inevitable victory of the proletariat, proved to be a less than helpful guide to action. It produced an immobilism, a passive wait for conditions to ripen, that opened up a disabling gulf between the party's revolutionary theory and its political practice. Or consider the phenomenon of fellow-travelling, in particular the way in which Western socialist intellectuals persuaded themselves in the 1930s that Stalinist Russia was a beacon of socialism. Without trying to explain this phenomenon, in all its genuine historical complexity, it can at least be said that it reflected the inheritance of a doctrinal tradition which taught that socialism was to be defined in terms of the abolition of private property and the socialization of the means of production, and that therefore the Soviet Union was 'essentially' a socialist society that had to be supported and defended by other socialists (even if this involved glossing over or averting the eyes from causes of disquiet). Indeed, throughout the 1930s, socialists reared in a theoretical tradition that promised both the inevitability of capitalist collapse and a historical schema in which socialism was the successor to capitalism were ill-equipped to negotiate that troublesome decade, even when they persuaded themselves (as the widespread appeal of Marxism testified) that they were singularly, indeed uniquely, well equipped. Their theory left no space for capitalist recovery and stabilization (which is why the reformers of capitalism, especially the social democratic ones, were so derided by their Marxist critics); and their understanding of fascism as essentially the death agony of monopoly capitalism ignored the possibility that it might be necessary to distinguish and defend capitalist democracy from something worse (instead of coupling fascism with the 'objective' social fascism of the social democrats, as communist doctrine and practice did at one stage). The refusal of the German communists to make common cause against Hitler is a stark reminder that doctrinal traditions carry with them consequences for political action, and inaction, in the real world.

If these are examples of particular consequences, some more general consequences and characteristics associated with the elevation of theory into the role of scientific (or quasi-scientific) doctrine may be identified. A basic but not insignificant point is that since scientific socialism requires scientific socialists, the effect is that advancement of orthodoxy becomes advancement of the bearers of that orthodoxy. Correct doctrine and its proper application are so central to the socialist project that a crucial role is given to the dealers in doctrine, whose superior understanding of the historical process enables them to lead a party that in turn will guide the masses in the appropriate political direction. Kautsky declared: 'Knowledge is still today a privilege of the property-owning classes: the proletariat cannot create out of itself a strong and living socialism. It must have it brought to it.' It will be necessary to return to this matter of 'consciousness from without' at a later stage; but for the moment it is enough to remember that a socialism that defines itself in terms of its possession of scientific knowledge carries with it a special authority for the possessors of that knowledge. It is an authority that has often been claimed, and converted into power.

There is an even more general, and more fundamental, characteristic associated with the theoretical tradition that claimed to base itself upon Marx's work. Marx advanced a pathbreaking theory of the long-term determinants of social structure and social change, but this was extended by the tradition that took his name into a science of immediate political action. Lichtheim makes this point well, in relation to Marx's class theory: 'This doctrine incorporated a highly original analysis applicable to long-run changes in the economic and social foundations of the political order. It thus provided an important tool for historians and sociologists concerned with the evolution of society since the sixteenth century, but it was useless as a guide to short-term political action.' Not merely could it not perform this role, but those who deployed it in this way converted a theory of long-run economic determination into a position that reduced politics to a branch of economics. Such 'reductionism' and 'economism' has been a central feature of the Marxist tradition, at least until recently. It has also sustained what Frank Parkin has ironically described as 'the Marxist science of predicting the past'.

This suggests a further problem. If a general theory of long-term social change was treated as a handbook of short-term political action, then the model of political economy provided by that theory, in its analysis of the dynamics of capitalism (and here the problem lies with its original formulation as much as with its subsequent use), was also treated as a doctrine of political consequences. In other words, a theory about value, falling profits, capitalist concentration, etc. (which may be more or less valid) was extended into a doctrine about the necessary political and social consequences of that theory (class conflict, consciousness, socialism). Yet this is an illegitimate and misleading extension, since the two domains are analytically distinct. Marx constructed a philosophical bridge between them, not an empirical one, and this bridge has been unable to support the weight of empirical evidence that has pressed down upon it. Even if Marx is acquitted of iron determinism there is *enough* economic determinism in his approach (what Engels was to describe as the *'ultimately* determining element') to leave too little space for the operation of other factors. Yet it is these 'other factors' that have intervened on so many different fronts to prevent Marx's political economy delivering its political consequences. Class consciousness has taken different forms, within particular societies and between societies, and has produced integration as well as resistance. The 'superstructure' of ideas, beliefs, social groupings, states, nationalisms, etc. has demonstrated a marked reluctance to be determined, and has evidenced a considerable ability to do some determining of its own (even, let it be whispered, of its economic base, as Stalin demonstrated in practice if not in theory). The point here, then, is not to ask the question why the theoretical model has failed to deliver the political goods (the painful and persistent question of so much contemporary Marxism), but to identify the flaw in an approach that invited such failure by believing that its theoretical model of capitalism was also a doctrine of political consequences for socialism. It was not, and the fact that it was not revealed its status to be, as Peter Worsley puts it, not a general science of *society* but 'a political economy that stopped short of becoming a sociology'. Or a politics, it should be added.

When democratic socialists have formulated their critique of traditional Marxism, they have wanted to deflate its scientific pretensions. While accepting in general terms Marx's account of the centrality of the mode of production and its class basis in explaining historical development and the broad structure of societies, democratic socialists have parted company with any thoroughgoing economic determinism. They have rejected it as inadequate history, and have wanted to assert a realm of at least partial independence for politics, values, and ideas (a realm that provides the arena for a democratic socialist politics). They have also challenged Marx's account of class polarization, working-class immiseration, and capitalist collapse; and have identified the practical failure of these and other Marxist expectations.

However, beyond these particular issues, there are two main lines of criticism. First, there is the effect that Marxism has had upon Marxists: they parrot the texts, reduce everything to rigid economic categories, believe they alone know how societies work, regard Marxism as a total, self-contained system, and exhibit a politics of arrogant intolerance (especially towards other, non-Marxist, socialists who are pityingly accused of 'idealism'). It is argued that these characteristics derive from the scientific status that the Marxist tradition has, falsely, claimed for itself.

The second main line of criticism from democratic socialists has centred on Marxism's lack of an ethical basis; indeed, its repudiation of the need for such a basis. Thus Lenin in 1920: 'We say that our morality is entirely subordinated to the interests of the proletariat's class struggle . . . Morality is what serves to destroy the old exploiting society and to unite all the working people around the proletariat, which is building up a new, a communist society . . . To a Communist all morality lies in this united discipline and conscious mass struggle against the exploiters. We do not believe in an eternal morality, and we expose the falseness of all the fables about morality.' This is a polemical statement, but represents the rejection of the need for an independent moral basis for socialism that has characterized the Marxist tradition. This position has been attacked by democratic socialists, partly because of the devaluation of the individual implied by the refusal to deal in anything but class categories, but also because of its fusion of the historically necessary and the morally desirable. All socialists might have as their objective a classless society, but there is a fundamental distinction between those who present this objective in terms of a scientific doctrine of historical immanence and those who regard it as a moral doctrine of the good society. Democratic socialists, taking their stand on the latter position, have therefore seen the Marxist tradition as providing an inadequate and unsatisfactory basis for socialism, despite its theoretical grandeur and comprehensive claims. As Bernard Crick has put it, 'theories of socialism without critical moral philosophy are as undesirable as they are impossible'. If the Marxist tradition has provided the source of socialism's most fertile theoretical work, it is the democratic socialist tradition that has developed its moral doctrine.

It should be said that in some sense this is a historical distinction, not least because of the variety of contemporary Marxisms. There is much less Marxist 'science' these days (notwithstanding M. Althusser, who managed to restore the scientific status of Marx's theory by banishing the empirical world altogether). Marx the 'humanist' has moved to centre stage, his work is presented more modestly as a fruitful method of analysis, and (picking up from the ideas of Antonio Gramsci, Italian Marxist theorist and an early leader of the Italian Communist Party) there is less economic determinism and more attention to the role of 'superstructural' elements and the importance of human subjectivity. These remarks of course do not apply to 'official' Marxism nor to much of Third World Marxism, but they do reflect the changing character of Marxism in the West. They may even reflect a process of the integration of Marxism into a broader democratic socialism, something that might have occurred much earlier but for the Bolshevik revolution. For the moment, though, it is still necessary to identify the different kinds of doctrine that have sustained different kinds of socialism.

Of course, socialism does require both positive doctrine and normative doctrine, empirical theory and moral philosophy. If a socialism without a moral doctrine is impossible, then a socialism without an empirical theory can become a mere fantasy. Yet the conversion of empirical theory into scientific doctrine has produced a contempt for the 'idealism' of a socialism of moral values. Similarly, some versions of 'moral' socialism have carried with them a contempt for theory. Both positions are inadequate, and have proved disabling in practice. However, to say that both kinds of doctrine are required by socialism is not to say that both are of equal status. There *is* a difference between a tradition that began life by believing (as Marx put it) that is was 'the riddle of history solved, and . . . knows itself to be that solution' and which continues to trade in a superior currency of essentialism, contradictions, and objectivism, and a tradition that offers a moral programme nourished by empirical theory. Perhaps William Morris's reported reply to the questioner who asked accusingly 'Does Comrade Morris accept Marx's Theory of Value?' was an attempt to explain this: 'To speak frankly, I do not know what Marx's Theory of Value is, and I'm damned if I want to know.'

4. Methods

What is generally called the ultimate goal of socialism is
nothing to me; the movement is everything.

Eduard Bernstein

If socialists have disagreed about the kind of doctrine that socialism essentially is, this disagreement has extended into further
differences concerning the means whereby socialist doctrines are
to be realized in practice. The two disagreements are closely connected. Thus when the 'revisionists' challenged the orthodoxies
of scientific socialism on the matter of the necessary collapse of
capitalism, this challenge implied not merely that socialist arguments had to be constructed on a different kind of doctrinal basis
but that the strategies and methods employed by socialists had
also to be revised.

Indeed, this was the political significance of that celebrated
dispute to its various protagonists. Revisionism implied reformism, while orthodoxy involved revolution. In fact, matters were
not quite as straightforward as this dichotomy suggests, for
reasons to be noticed shortly, but it was nevertheless inevitable
that arguments about economic doctrine should extend into
arguments about political method. If the breakdown of capitalism was just around the corner of history, and if socialism
and barbarism were the only alternatives in this situation,
then the revolutionary assumption of power by the proletariat
was an integral part of the historical prospectus. However, if
there was nothing inevitable about capitalism's collapse, if it was
capable of stabilization and adjustment, then socialism would
need to develop a reformist strategy linking state action and electoral pressure. It is clear then that arguments about methods do
not stand alone, but are intimately related to wider socialist
positions.

It should also be evident that socialists have argued for, and
practised, a variety of methods in pursuit of their objectives.
Although this variety is frequently compressed into familiar

categories marked 'reform' and 'revolution', such compression does scant justice to the modalities of these terms while obscuring from view other dimensions of the argument about methods. It has been possible to be a reformer without also becoming a reformist. There have been revolutionary socialists who have organized for reform, just as there have been non-revolutionary socialists who have allowed for the possibility of revolution. Parliamentary socialism does not necessarily exclude other, extra-parliamentary forms of action. Some socialists have rejected violence; others have embraced it. Some have emphasized the need for disciplined organization; others the need for spontaneity. There have been insurrectionists, and revolutionaries who have denounced insurrectionism. Socialists have sought to capture the state, and to destroy it. Political action has been opposed by industrial action. Political action for economic purposes has been matched by industrial action for political purposes. Then there have been those socialists who have sought to point the way forward by constructing experiments in practical socialism within and alongside capitalism.

It is possible to identify these different approaches throughout socialism's history. By the middle of the nineteenth century the main positions, the basis for subsequent traditions, were already in evidence. There was a 'communism' that was revolutionary and insurrectionary, associated with the names of Babeuf and Buonarroti, the extreme left wing of the French Revolution; and which found its continuing expression in the insurrectionary activities of Blanqui and his apostles of revolutionary vanguardism ('Blanquism'). There were 'utopian' socialists who thought that the reform of society could be effected by enlightened legislation and rational legislators (the Saint-Simonian tradition), or who sought, like the Fourierists and Owenites, to found small communities on the basis of their principles of social reconstruction. There were socialists, like Louis Blanc, who laid the basis for a reformism that involved forming alliances and securing parliamentary victories, and which was extended by Lassalle in Germany into a strategy of electoral organization and state action. There were also other socialists, like Proudhon, who in their espousal of direct action by producers nourished anarchist and syndicalist traditions that rejected 'political' socialism and parliamentarism in favour of the self-emancipation of industrial militancy.

When Marx set out to conquer the workers' movement with his

ideas, it was against this background of competing strategies. He had to transcend them theoretically, and defeat them practically. What this involved can be seen in a number of ways: for example, in his brushing aside of the utopians and his attack on the intellectual poverty of Proudhon, the struggle against Bakunin and the anarchists, the distancing from the primitiveness of Blanquism, and the repudiation of Lassalle. By the final quarter of the nineteenth century, Marx's ideas had achieved a theoretical supremacy within the workers' movement, and this was converted into a practical supremacy when the German Marxists deployed their Marxism as the organizing ideology of their own movement and then of the Second International. Some aspects of what this involved have been discussed already, but it was clearly of central significance that the main body of the European socialist movement adopted the strategic perspective of Marxism. The developing labour movement required a theoretical underpinning and Marxism supplied it. However, this in turn required that Marxism should demonstrate the much heralded unity of its theory and practice. When it met the labour movement, its status was not merely that of a theory to be subscribed to, but of a strategy to be acted upon. But what was that strategy?

The history of the Second International period testifies to the difficulties lurking behind that simple question. However, these difficulties cannot be separated from the treatment of socialist methods to be found in Marx's own work. The centrality of revolution in Marx's theory is clear, yet despite its centrality there is no extended discussion of the character of the revolutionary process, and this reflects the general absence of a developed theory of politics. Marx's model of social change had revolution at its centre because it was rooted in a conflict theory of society. It presented society as the scene of a class antagonism that was inevitable and irreconcilable, even when it did not assume the form of open warfare and despite the fact that it was wrapped around with layers of ideological mystification. Marx's production theory of society made class conflict the motor of social change, a motor that worked through revolutions (of more or less violence). The revolutionary 'communism' of the early Marx, as expressed in the call to arms of the *Manifesto*, might give way to the long-term structural perspectives of the later Marx, as seen in the *Grundrisse*, where the revolutionary agency slips from view, but revolution as the method of social change remains constant and integral.

However, this still leaves open the question of what Marx actually understood by revolution. Some help here may be derived from the gynaecological imagery he frequently employed when discussing the transition from one form of society to another. This is the imagery of wombs, embryos, and midwives, in which new societies are born out of old ones after a suitable period of gestation, and through the agency of an appropriately qualified midwife. Societies are in a condition of perpetual pregnancy, giving birth when they come to ripeness (the exception being socialism, of course, which represents the final discovery of an effective method of social contraception). This imagery does reflect an account of social change that turns on the developing relationship between the forces and relations of production, and in which productive 'fetters' have to be broken when new societies are born. What this meant was that revolution was as inevitable and necessary as childbirth but was likewise to be understood as one moment in a larger and longer process. It was the moment of 'break', when the new was created out of the old, but was to be seen as the culmination of a whole process of social formation. Like childbirth, it was likely to be a painful moment, but it was the pain of transcendence and release.

At risk of exhausting the imagery, Marx's understanding of revolution also carried with it a warning of the dangers of prematurity. If social revolutions were to be understood as one moment in a process of social development, it was unscientific to believe that they could be precipitated in situations where the necessary conditions did not exist or were undeveloped. This was Marx's charge against the insurrectionism of the Blanquists, those 'alchemists of revolution' who believed that 'the only condition for the revolution is a sufficient organisation of their own conspiracy'. According to Engels, the Blanquists believed 'in the principle that revolutions do not make themselves, but are made; that they are made by a comparatively small minority and according to a previously designed plan; and finally, that the time is always ripe'. However, even such warnings against the revolutionary alchemism of unscientific quacks do not serve fully to identify Marx's own position.

If revolution, properly understood, was the motor of social

change in Marx's general theory, this did not prevent him from
supporting demands for particular social reforms within the
existing order or from attaching himself to the cause of democratic republics founded upon universal suffrage. The perspective, however, remained tactical, turning on the relationship
between social and democratic reform and the longer-term process of class conflict and revolution. It was a perspective that was
decisively influenced by Marx's analysis of the state, an analysis
that combined an essentialist position ('merely the organised
power of one class for oppressing another') in terms of his general theory with a series of modifications and qualifications in
relation to particular state forms. This combination again
reflected the absence of a developed theory of politics (and
explains why later Marxists have had to spend so much time and
energy trying to construct one). The result, in terms of political
method, was that Marx presented violent revolution as the model
of social change (in the words of *Capital*, 'force is the midwife of
every old society pregnant with a new one'), but at the same time,
in the *obiter dicta* of his maturity, seemed to allow the possibility
that a route of peaceful constitutionalism might be available to
the working class in some countries. The most celebrated of such
obiter dicta is Marx's reported speech in Amsterdam in 1872: 'We
know of the allowances we must make for the institutions, cus-
toms and traditions of the various countries; and we do not deny
that there are countries such as America, England, and I would
add Holland if I knew your institutions better, where the working
people may achieve their goal by peaceful means. If that is true,
we must also recognise that in most of the continental countries it
is force that will have to be the lever of our revolutions.'

Even this brief sketch of Marx's approach is enough to reveal
that it provided a profoundly ambiguous legacy. It offered an
account of the state as essentially a class agency, yet was
accompanied by accounts of actual states that suggested the difficulties with such essentialism. It demonstrated the need for the
workers' movement to destroy the state, but also the tactics for
using it. It announced the necessity of forceful revolution, but
also introduced a doctrine of exceptionalism. When combined
with the areas of crucial neglect (for example, the role of parties,
their relation to classes, the nature of political leadership), this
was an elusive political methodology. When further combined,

as the next chapter shows, with the absence of any sustained discussion of the political structure of socialist society, it became an even more elusive guide to socialist politics. All this may be regarded as a necessary and unsurprising consequence of a theoretical position that, when the relevant qualifications have been registered, gave a secondary and derivative status to politics. However, it also meant that when the meaning of 'revolution' was debated during the Second International period, or when Lenin argued the need to 'smash' the state as good Marxist orthodoxy, it was possible to conscript Marx into competing positions on the battle lines.

It was against this background that the 'revolution versus reform' controversy within German Social Democracy took shape. Here was a Marxist party (its Marxism given popular form in its 1891 Erfurt Programme) committed to a revolutionary doctrine but engaged in the electoral and parliamentary politics of reform. This story is usually told in terms of the dangerous, and ultimately fatal, gulf between theory and practice that this involved (a gulf down which European socialism was to fall in 1914). While such a story is clearly true, there are disputes about who its villains are and what alternative endings were available. Lenin, of course, was to use the experience as an object-lesson in the rottenness of European social democracy, revealed as essentially reformist behind its cloak of revolutionary rhetoric, and now to be opposed by a genuinely revolutionary communism. However, this was a retrospective discovery on Lenin's part, signalled by his invention of the 'renegade' Kautsky. During the heyday of the Second International Lenin had bowed before the authority of Kautsky as the defender of a correct Marxist revolutionary line against both reformists and insurrectionists, a strategic perspective which was rooted in a scientific understanding of the laws of social development. As Kautsky had put it: 'The task of Social Democracy consists, not in bringing about the inevitable catastrophe, but in delaying it as long as possible, that is to say, in avoiding with care anything that could resemble a provocation or the appearance of a provocation.'

In *The Road to Power* (1909) Kautsky had distinguished, as the leading theorist of scientific socialism, between a revolutionary party and a revolution-making party: 'Social democracy is a revolutionary party, but not a revolution-making party. We know that our objective can only be reached through revolution. But we also know that it is no more in our power to make this revolution than it is in the power of our enemies to prevent it. We have no wish either to stir up revolution or to prepare the ground for one.' Such formulations may now, with hindsight, appear to give the game away, reducing revolution to a metaphor and providing a rhetorical camouflage for political passivity, but it should also be remembered how accurately they reflected the doctrinal atmosphere of Second International scientific socialism. This involved waiting for the maturation of capitalism, which, in turn, would inevitably deliver socialism. There would necessarily be a revolutionary moment, but it was the evolutionary process at work that really mattered for it was this that would ensure that when the revolutionary break came the balance of forces would be such as to guarantee a swift and painless victory. From this perspective, then, it was perfectly possible, indeed necessary, to be both reformer and revolutionary.

In fact, of course, it meant that one was neither a coherent reformer nor a coherent revolutionary. To be the former would involve thinking through the implications of an electoral road to socialism, while to be the latter would involve some consideration of how 'maturity' was to be judged and how revolutionary consciousness and activity were to be actively promoted in order to connect with the maturing conditions. This dilemma, and the need for a clear choice of strategy, was perceived in their sharply different ways by both the 'revisionist' Bernstein and the 'radical' Luxemburg. In challenging the scientific status of key elements of Marxist doctrine, and therefore also their inevitabilist implications, Bernstein argued for a view of socialism as a process that was already underway and could be carried forward indefinitely by democratic reformism. In 1898 he wrote:

It is my firm conviction that the present generation will already see realised a large part of socialism, if not in official form, at least in content. The constant enlargement of social duties, i.e. of the duties and corresponding rights of the individual against society and of the duties of society to the individual, the extension of the right of society, as organised in the nation or the state, to supervise economic life, the construction of democratic self-government at village, district and provincial levels, and the extension of the tasks of these associations—and that for me is development towards socialism.

It was in this sense that Bernstein could declare that for him the 'ultimate goal' of socialism was nothing and the 'movement' everything. Building socialism was a continuous process, not a single, dramatic cataclysm.

Bernstein's view was met with a chorus of denunciation from the guardians of Marxist orthodoxy. Perhaps this really derived from a sense that Bernstein had simply theorized the practice of the Social Democrats, confronting them with the fact that they were in reality a party of reform even if they remained formally attached to a doctrine of revolution. Even Engels, in his much discussed preface to a new edition of Marx's *Class Struggles in France*, which he wrote in 1895 not long before his death, seemed to have provided a decisive endorsement of the constitutional road. Declaring that 'the mode of struggle of 1848 is today obsolete from every point of view', Engels proclaimed the advantages of electoral politics and eulogized the advance of German Social Democracy as a model for others:

Its growth proceeds as spontaneously, as steadily, as irresistibly, and at the same time as tranquilly as a natural process. All government interventions have proved powerless against it. We can count even today on two and a half million voters. If it continues in this fashion, by the end of the century we shall conquer the greater part of the middle section of society, petty bourgeois and small peasants, and grow into the decisive power in the land, before which all other powers will have to bow, whether they like it or not. To keep this growth going without interruption until of itself it gets beyond the control of the ruling governmental system, not to fritter away this daily increasing shock force in advance guard fighting, but to keep it intact until the day of the decision, that is our main task . . . The irony of world history turns everything upside down. We, the 'revolutionaries', the 'rebels'—we are thriving far better on legal methods than on illegal methods and revolt. The parties of order, as they call themselves, are perishing under the legal conditions created by themselves.

The ambiguity remained (there would still be 'the day of the decision', and the party of order would throw over legalism when this became necessary) but Engels had clearly extended Marx's allowance of particular exceptions to the revolutionary norm into a general vindication of constitutional politics as the appropriate socialist method at the end of the nineteenth century. This was not a theoretical discovery, but a recognition of the actual role

that mass socialist parties were now playing in the political life of
West European societies. They were framing practical pro-
grammes of reform and campaigning for electoral support on the
basis of them. As Bebel, the German SPD leader, expressed it:
'The heart of the people turns towards us because we take up the
cause of their daily needs.' Here was a process of integration into
'normal' politics that could not easily be combined with a commitment to overthrow the political system itself. How far such
integration could go was thrown into sharp relief in France in
1898, when a socialist accepted ministerial office in a bourgeois
government; and this 'Millerand case' sent shock waves through
international socialism. In general terms, it looked increasingly
implausible that, in a theoretical sense, a tactic of reform was
organically connected to a strategy of revolution. As Joll com-
ments, in his history of the Second International: 'It is very hard
to work for the overthrow of existing society if one is stopping by
the way to improve the drainage system or the transport service.'

There were those who, like Bernstein, recognized the developing gap between revolutionary theory and reformist practice
within social democracy but, unlike Bernstein, sought to close the
gap by amending the practice in the direction of the theory. This
was the position of the radical left wing of German social democracy, represented pre-eminently by Rosa Luxemburg; and of the
equivalent wing of the Second International itself, represented
above all by Lenin. Both Luxemburg and Lenin fell in behind
Kautsky in his rebuttal of revisionism and later they were both to
mount attacks on the leadership of social democracy; but also on
each other. Luxemburg's *Social Reform or Revolution* (1899)
was a sustained polemic against Bernstein's revisionism and its
reformist implications, and an assertion of the view that reforms
had no value or meaning except as part of a strategy of revolution. There could be no legal route to socialism because the domination of capital was essentially an extra-legal phenomenon.
Thus reform and revolution were 'not different methods of historic development that can be picked out at pleasure from the
counter of history, just as one chooses hot or cold sausages', but
represented different kinds of activity with intrinsically different
objectives:

That is why people who pronounce themselves in favour of the method
of legislative reform *in place* of and in *contradistinction to* the conquest

of political power and social revolution, do not really choose a more tranquil, calmer and slower road to the *same* goal, but a *different* goal. Instead of taking a stand for the establishment of a new society, they take a stand for surface modifications of the old society. If we follow the political conceptions of revisionism, we arrive at the same conclusion that is reached when we follow the economic theories of revisionism. Our programme becomes not the realisation of *socialism*, but the reform of *capitalism*; not the suppression of the system of wage labour, but the diminution of exploitation, that is, the suppression of the abuses of capitalism instead of the suppression of capitalism itself.

Luxemburg's attack on the theoretical revisionism of Bernstein later extended into an assault on the practical reformism of the SPD leadership. Having a profound belief in the revolutionary potential of the working class, she berated a political style that stifled the development of revolutionary consciousness rather than actively promoted it. Her advocacy of the mass strike as a political weapon, a lesson she drew from the events of 1905 in Russia, epitomized her belief in the 'spontaneity' of proletarian self-emancipation. Following Marx, Luxemburg believed that the proletariat could and would emancipate itself through a genuine revolution of the masses. On the one hand, this led her into opposition to the revisionists and centrists of social democracy, but it also involved a rejection of the Leninist organizational model of revolution that turned on the role of the vanguard party. Instead of a dynamic and 'dialectical' relationship between party and class, leaders and masses, Leninism represented 'a mechanical transfer of the organisational principles of the Blanquistic movement of conspiratorial groups to the Social Democratic movement of the working masses'.

Where Luxemburg and Lenin were in agreement was in their attribution of responsibility for the socialist débâcle of 1914 to the leadership of the social democratic movement. They both believed that revolutions had to be made (albeit in rather different ways), not waited for; and their charge against the pre-1914 social democratic leadership was that it played a waiting game that both concealed its actual relapse into reformism and atrophied the working-class movement. Just as Kautsky had been able to draw upon a reading of Marx to sustain an evolutionary perspective of maturation and ripeness in which revolution as activity faded from view, so Lenin was able (notably in his *State and Revolution*, written on the eve of the Bolshevik revolution) to draw with no less credibility upon an alternative reading in which the transition to socialism took the form of a revolutionary push in which states were smashed, oppositions crushed, and political violence liberally deployed. There could be no truck with the fraud of parliamentary democracy: 'To decide once every few years which member of the ruling class is to repress and crush the people through parliament—this is the real essence of bourgeois parliamentarism, not only in parliamentary—constitutional monarchies, but also in the most democratic republics.' Revolution was on the socialist agenda, no longer as a metaphor, and as the only item.

Lenin had satisfied himself, as seen in the previous chapter, that the objective conditions for global revolution had been established and so set about the business of lighting the Russian spark. His success in this task, on the basis of the organizational principles he hammered out, has provided the foundation for the (communist) claim that Leninism represents the extension of Marxism into the age of revolution (an extension henceforth to be sanctified as 'Marxism-Leninism'). In essence, the claim was—and still is—that Leninists are professionals in the business of revolution-making. It was this professionalism that was supposed to be passed on to the communist parties that were established throughout Europe by the Third International, with the task of saving the working class of these countries from the degeneracy of social democracy and providing them with revolutionary leadership. When the international revolution failed to materialize (despite a number of revolutionary outbreaks in the immediate post-1918 period, and a widespread panic among European governments about the contaminating spread of Bolshevism), socialism was left in its disabling state of polarization between a 'revolutionary' communism and a 'reformist' social democracy.

Perhaps two footnotes to the account of pre-1914 social democracy should be entered. The first concerns syndicalism; the second relates to British socialism. The former rejected the whole business of bourgeois parliamentarism and political action in favour of direct action by the producers. The latter was overwhelmingly parliamentary and constitutionalist. Both addressed themselves to the matter of reformism: one to denounce it, the other to embrace it. The French syndicalist philosopher Georges Sorel was preoccupied with the debilitating effect of parliamentarism on working-class militancy, in its encouragement of ideas of compromise and social peace ('the reconciliation of contraries in the equivocations of the professors'). The need was to promote working-class violence, heroism, and authenticity if it was to perform its conquering role, and this was to be effected by means of the general strike, the heroic 'myth' of the proletariat. Its function was not to win particular victories, but to clarify, mobilize, and polarize: 'the idea of the general strike has such power behind it that it drags into the revolutionary track everything it touches.' Even though it would be misleading to present Sorel as the representative theorist of syndicalism, the advocacy and practice of producer militancy as an alternative to 'political' socialism have provided a continuing, if minority, answer to the question of socialist method. The strategy of 'encroaching control' in industry advocated by the guild socialists in Britain may be seen as one version of this general approach.

If syndicalism stood outside the mainstream of Second International scientific socialism, then so too in a sharply different way did British socialism as a whole. Both the moralism of the ethical socialists and the rationalism of the Fabians reinforced the commitment to constitutionalism. The ethical socialists rejected any resort to violence and addressed themselves to moral persuasion and parliamentary agitation. As Keir Hardie frequently expressed it, they were waging war not upon a class but upon a system. Meanwhile, the Fabians were confidently demonstrating (on grounds that seem to have influenced Bernstein) why revolution was unnecessary and why a process of reform that was already well underway could gradually transform capitalist individualism into socialist collectivism. Concluding his contribution to *Fabian Essays* on 'The Transition to Social Democracy', Bernard Shaw reviewed the character of 'the humdrum programme of the practical Social Democrat today' and announced:

There is not one new item in it. All are applications of principles already admitted, and extensions of practices already in full activity. All have on them that stamp of the vestry which is so congenial to the British mind. None of them compel the use of the words Socialism or Revolution: at no point do they involve guillotining, declaring the Rights of Man, swearing on the altar of the country, or anything else that is supposed to be essentially un-English. And they are all sure to come—landmarks on our course already visible to far-sighted politicians even of the party which dreads them.

It was not necessary to admire this 'sordid, slow, reluctant, cowardly path to justice' with its 'paltry instalments of betterment'; but it was necessary to accept that it had rendered obsolete an earlier socialist catastrophism.

Having mapped out some of the leading positions on the matter of socialist methods that had staked their claim by the fateful second decade of this century, it is now possible to offer some observations in the light of subsequent experience. It is difficult to avoid the conclusion that each strategy has failed to deliver the goods. The Kautskian perspective of capitalist maturation reaching the point at which socialism would step into its place could scarcely account for the continuance of a chronic over-ripeness. The Leninist perspective of global revolution had its doctrinal basis cut away the day after it was born, and in its practical application has failed to deliver revolution anywhere in Western Europe. The reformist perspective has been able to win power and deliver reforms, but it has nowhere been able to deliver what any of the assorted pre-1914 protagonists would have regarded as socialism. Syndicalism and its derivatives expired as an effective movement in the aftermath of the First World War. To complete the picture, the polarization that was enforced upon the labour movement not merely weakened it, but closed off options of theory and strategy that might have been available to it.

The murder of Rosa Luxemburg in 1919 symbolized the closure of a non-Leninist revolutionary option (whether or not this was a viable option, when separated from the belief in an essentially revolutionary proletariat, is another matter). The Bolshevik appropriation of Marxism ossified it as a body of theory and, for at least a generation, effectively closed it off as a creative source of socialist strategy. In its communist version, it became an instrument whereby Moscow sought to dress up its line to its satellite parties in the legitimating cloak of scientific socialist doctrine (all the more necessary when this line was so manifestly inappropriate to the domestic situations these parties faced, and when the line was quite likely to be reversed overnight). On the non-communist side, the need to withstand the attacks from the communists pushed many socialists into a narrower and less adventurous form of social democracy than they might otherwise have wished; but in conditions of polarization they had nowhere else to go. Since 1945 some revision in this picture has become necessary, but not of a kind to alter its basic shape.

A revolutionary socialism has chalked up some successes, but in places, forms, and methods a million miles away from the revolutionary prospectus offered by classical Marxism. This remains true in spite of the mobilization of Marxism as socialists' ideology, and their deployment of Leninism as a revolutionary manual. Lenin's demonstration that socialists can make revolutions in unlikely places, given sufficient discipline and organization, stands confirmed. But can they make them in likely places, in the heartlands of developed capitalism, as the classical Marxist tradition envisaged? Here the story since 1945 looks entirely different. Not only did social democracy become more securely reformist in this period (symbolized by the revised doctrinal basis adopted by the German SPD in 1959 at Bad Godesberg), but more secure on the Left. Moreover, there was a striking development in the character of West European communism in this period. Lenin had blamed the failure of European revolution on the reformism of social democratic leaders, and had established communist parties that would give the working classes of Europe an authentic revolutionary leadership. It became an axiom of the communist tradition that reformist social democracy, in the form of leaders who betrayed their class' and were wedded to bourgeois parliamentarism, was the chief obstacle to revolution in the West.

Yet the evolution of communist parties in Western Europe in the past two decades (most notably in Italy, most slowly in France) has been precisely in the direction of reformism and constitutionalism, carrying with it a disavowal of any revolutionary intent. Moreover, this stance of 'Eurocommunism' is presented not as a device to avoid frightening the children (i.e. the electors), but as a positive commitment to the political institutions of bourgeois democracy. As Carrillo, the Spanish communist theorist of this new revisionism, put it, 'the political system established in Western Europe, based on representative political institutions—parliament, political and philosophical pluralism, the theory of the separation of powers, decentralisation, human rights, etc.—. . . is in essentials valid'. Eurocommunists would respect this 'essential validity' both in their pursuit of political power and in their exercise of it. All this is clearly a long way from Leninism, and from the role assigned to these parties by Lenin. It is also very close to social democracy, as the left-wing critics of Eurocommunism like to point out (to one such critic, Ernest Mandel, it is 'incontestable . . . that Eurocommunism today is repeating the reasoning of social democracy yesterday word for word'). Of course, this is strenuously denied by the Eurocommunists, as with Carrillo's distinction between a Eurocommunism that aims to 'transform' capitalism and a social democracy that merely wants to 'administer' it. It is argued that there are different kinds of reformism, a kind that means business and a kind that does not, even though they may look similar. The difference lies in the fact (as Miliband explains in his account of *Marxism and Politics*) that 'on any realistic view' the leaders of social democracy must be 'reckoned as forming part, and a very important part, of the conservative forces of advanced capitalist countries'. Thus the embarrassment caused by the existence of rival reformisms, Marxist and social democratic, is overcome once it is understood that, objectively speaking, social democrats are really playing for the other side. At least some things in the Marxist universe remain the same.

However, there are also other problems raised by the new tendencies. Why is the political structure of Western democracy to be regarded as 'valid' now, when its invalidity from a Marxist perspective had been proclaimed for so long? Why has revolution become unnecessary, when its indispensability at some point was traditionally regarded as axiomatic? In pondering upon such questions, it should be recalled that in the Marxist tradition the issue of socialist methods in relation to reformism, parliamentary action, etc. has presented itself as a problem of *tactics*. In other words, the political apparatus of capitalist democracy had no intrinsic merit except in so far as it might offer new tactical opportunities for Marxist strategists. Indeed, its absence of intrinsic merit was an article of faith, and Marxists were constantly stripping off its sham democratic veneer to reveal the class oppression just underneath (as with Arthur Scargill's claim during the 1984–5 miners' strike that the activities of the police clearly revealed how behind its democratic façade Britain is 'really' a police state). Marxist discussion turned on the extent to which bourgeois parliamentarism could be *used* for socialist purposes. It was in this spirit that Marx had discussed the matter, and in which the discussion continued thereafter (including, for example, Lenin's polemic in 1920 against ultra-left anti-parliamentarism in his *'Left-Wing' Communism—An Infantile Disorder*). Against this background the Eurocommunist discovery of the 'validity' of Western democracy represented a departure, although to some it looked rather belated and grudging while to others its significance as a conversion was somewhat devalued by the extent to which it still looked suspiciously like a tactical response.

The twin discoveries that there were different kinds of reformism, and that Western democracy was valuable in itself, could scarcely come as a revelation to democratic socialists. They had been advancing these positions, from within the social democratic tradition, for at least half a century. It was possible for pre-1914 social democracy to assume that socialism would extend and incorporate the inheritance of liberal democracy into its own structures, for this was built into its developmental model of social change. This assumption was no longer possible after 1917, which meant that liberal democracy had either to be denounced as a fraud (as it was by the communists) or embraced as a value (as it was by the social democrats). If 'social democracy' now came to mean a clearly reformist position, whether used in a pejorative or approbatory sense, it also came to signify to its adherents a policy of completing democracy by extending it from the political and civic sphere into the social and economic. In its existing form it was not hollow, as the Marxists tended to argue, but incomplete. Similarly, 'democratic socialism' was coined to describe a position that was committed to socialism, but was also committed to democracy as both the method of change and the structural form of socialist society. During the twentieth century it became important for some socialists at least to make such matters clear.

Bolshevism demonstrated that it was perfectly possible for socialism to be undemocratic; while fascism demonstrated that it was equally possible for capitalist democracy to turn into something infinitely worse. The range of historical options there-fore expanded beyond the neat categories of pre-1914 scientific socialism. This caused democratic socialists to define their rela-tionship, at least in respect of their own societies, to the inheri-tance of liberal democracy. This inheritance was to be regarded as a considerable achievement, and socialism was to be regarded as a further development of the same civilizing tradition. Further, this was not merely a matter of political theory but a reflection of the growth and diffusion of a democratic political culture. R. H. Tawney, writing in the 1930s, identified what a political culture 'steeped for two centuries in a liberal tradition' meant for social-ism in Britain:

The result is the existence of a body of opinion, larger, probably, than in most other countries, which is sensitive on such subjects as personal liberty, freedom of speech and meeting, tolerance, the exclusion of vio-lence from politics, parliamentary government—what, broadly, it regards as fair play and the guarantees for it. The only version of social-ism which, as things are today, has the smallest chance of winning mass support, is one which accepts that position. Its exponents must realise that the class which is the victim of economic exploitation, instead of merely reading about it, is precisely the class which attaches most impor-tance to these elementary decencies. They must face the fact that, if the public, and particularly the working-class public, is confronted with the choice between capitalist democracy, with all its nauseous insincerities, and undemocratic socialism, it will choose the former every time. They must make it clear beyond the possibility of doubt that the socialist commonwealth which they preach will be built on democratic founda-tions. That fact is a proof, not of stupidity, but of intelligence. It means that Henry Dubb has the sense to prefer two good things to one . . . In becoming a socialist, he has no intention of surrendering his rights as a citizen, which after all, he once fought pretty hard to win. But, whether admirable or regrettable, that mentality remains a fact. Any realist strat-egy must be based upon it.

Tawney's point, it should be noticed, was not merely that it was tactically necessary to take account of the views of Henry Dubb, but that Henry Dubb was right. However, to adopt a posi-tion of this kind did not also require that democratic socialists should become political innocents. The method to which they committed themselves was only advanced as appropriate to those societies with a tradition and practice of political democracy. Where democracy· did not exist, or was flouted, then other methods became available. In particular, if a democratic socialist government found itself subverted by unconstitutional opposition then it would be fully entitled to answer in kind. The fear, or even expectation, of such subversion was widely expressed and debated on the British Left in the 1930s (so much so that in 1932 the impeccably moderate Clement Attlee, future prime minister, was to be found suggesting that socialists should train people to take over command positions in the armed forces in anticipation of such an eventuality). The ability of the 1945 Labour Government to fulfil its programme could therefore be regarded as a vindication of the viability of a democratic socialist strategy (in G. D. H. Cole's phrase, the answer to the Marxists was now 'in the facts'). However, there was no more reason for democratic socialists than for Marxists to be surprised that a democratically elected Marxist government should be ousted by a coup (as in Chile) or that the prospect of a socialist party coming to power in a general election should be pre-empted by a military takeover (as happened in Greece).

If democratic socialists might regard themselves as having a rather more durable claim to the title than the new breed of 'democratic' communists, they also know a thing or two about the varieties of reformism. In its reaction against communism, and its firm embrace of liberal democracy, social democracy has certainly been prone to slacken its socialist resolve. The history of this tendency is there to be seen in both its theoretical development and its exercise of office. It has frequently shown a capacity for degeneration into mere electoralism and governmentalism, making it implausible to claim, except in a rhetorical sense, that its reforming endeavours were part of a wider strategy of social transformation. However, this is not enough to sustain the charge that social democracy is in a generic sense, always and everywhere, a support for capitalism rather than a democratic challenge to it (unless, that is, a mode of analysis is employed in which this is necessarily the case). The historical evidence suggests that social democracy has taken different forms and been capable of delivering different results. It has not delivered 'socialism' of course, but it may be that the time perspective in which such delivery has traditionally been envisaged should be radically revised. It may be a case of going on going on.

However, if this is so then it requires a clear sense of destination and strategy or it does issue in *mere* reformism and accommodative integration. Here again those democratic socialists who have constituted the left wing of social democracy could reasonably claim to have kept this perspective alive. Moreover, their advocacy of the democratic method has been coupled with a vigorous and expansive sense of what this involves in terms of political action. It means as Tawney put it, thinking of democracy not merely as a political mechanism but as 'a force to be released'. It does not mean a retreat into a political passivity, but requires the mobilization of a people. Thus while a Marxist might, like Miliband, attend to the 'considerable constraints' imposed on revolutionary movements by bourgeois constitutionalism, a democratic socialist like Aneurin Bevan emphasizes the tremendous opportunities offered by parliamentary democracy for socialist political action. However, these opportunities have to be exploited to the full, through relentless democratic energy, or vacillation and lassitude will result. In Bevan's words, 'audacity is the mood that should prevail among Socialists as they apply the full armament of democratic values to the problems of the times'. In other words, democratic socialism gives a particular importance to the character and quality of political action; which may explain why Marxists have traditionally regarded this position and its practitioners with such theoretical pity.

There is a final general point here, arising out of these remarks on democratic socialism. It concerns the relationship between socialist means and ends. Democratic socialism, as was seen, contains an argument about both socialist means and socialist ends, and the necessary relationship between them. It is possible, as has also been seen, to take a rather different view of this matter, whereby the choice of means is regarded instrumentally and tactically, and where (for example, with Lenin) it becomes perfectly possible to combine a revolution effected by means of the iron discipline of a vanguard party with a post-revolutionary prospectus of stateless democracy. Such a disassociation of political means and ends not only seems unlikely, but has all the weight of historical evidence against it. In other words, it is the case not only that political means and ends *should* be related, but that they *are*. If parliamentary, constitutional socialism has (so far) only produced social democracy, then revolutionary socialism has (so far) only produced state authoritarianism. Rosa

Luxemburg was clearly right: socialist methods cannot be freely chosen—like hot or cold sausages—from the counter of history. The menu you choose does affect the sort of meal you are likely to get.

5. Structures

To my mind, there have always been two fundamental
cleavages in socialist thought—the cleavage between
revolutionaries and reformists, and the cleavage between
centralisers and federalists.

G. D. H. Cole

If the antagonism between reform and revolution is a familiar
theme in the history of socialism, the same is not true of the
arguments about the structural form of socialism. These arguments tend to be reduced to accounts of the distracting difficulties caused to mainstream socialism at various periods by the
activities of anarchists and syndicalists. Yet, at the end of the
twentieth century, questions concerning the structural principles
and shape of socialism are once again at the centre of socialist
discussion. This suggests the need to identify some of the arguments, issues, and traditions.

It may help to clear some ground if the reasons for the contemporary interest in these matters are frankly acknowledged. In his
magisterial account of the development of Marxism, Kolakowski
remarks on 'the strange fate of an idea which began in Promethean humanism and culminated in the monstrous tyranny of
Stalin'. Leaving aside (at least for the moment) the implied
derivation of Stalin from Marx, this remark may be extended to
socialism as a whole. Early-nineteenth-century socialism was,
in its various forms, libertarian, democratic, communitarian,
and self-managing. These forms are represented by Proudhon's
mutualism, Fourier's *phalanstères*, the Owenite experiments in
co-operative living, the Saint-Simonian substitution of the
administration of things by producers for the government of men
by politicians; and, of course, by the comprehensive prospectus
for human emancipation offered by Marx. By contrast, late-
twentieth-century socialism has come to be associated on all sides
with centralism and statism.

This association may be seen as relatively benign (liberal social democracy) or as positively malign (authoritarian communism), but either way the association is there. Twentieth-century communism has invented the monolithic party dictatorship as the organizational model of socialism. Twentieth-century social democracy, through its chosen method of piling ever more powers and responsibilities upon the state, has been the architect of the modern bureaucratic welfare state. Both roads have clearly led socialism a long way from that original vision of a stateless communism. By the 1940s, Schumpeter could declare (in his *Capitalism, Socialism and Democracy*) that 'what may be termed Centralist Socialism seems to me to hold the field so clearly that it would be waste of space to consider other forms'. These 'other forms' were now judged to have become historically, and technologically, obsolete, with the advocates of a non-statist, associational socialism shunted to the political sidelines. One such advocate was G. D. H. Cole, who concluded his vast survey of the *History of Socialist Thought* at the end of the 1950s with the lonely affirmation that he was 'neither a Communist nor a Social Democrat, because I regard both as creeds of centralisation and bureaucracy'.

A generation later, though, both the radical Right and the radical Left are united in their aversion to the state. However, while the Right has a clear sense of what the displacement of the state involves (for example, in terms of deregulation, denationalization, private markets in welfare, more freedom to become unequal) and what it does *not* involve (above all, any reduction in the political power of the state, but rather the intensification of such power), the Left seems to encounter greater difficulties in giving content to an alternative version of socialism. Unlike the Right, it is prepared to curtail the state's political power in the name of democratic accountability and civil liberty, but finds it much more difficult to develop a non-centralist version of a socialist economy. It is significant that, at the end of the twentieth century, state socialism seems to have few friends on the contemporary Left in the West; but it is equally significant that the shape of an alternative form of socialism remains elusive, both theoretically and practically.

Some of the reasons for the development of socialism-as-statism can be briefly identified. These range from the particular circumstances in which the world's first socialist revolution took place, a revolution of backwardness organized by a disciplined party, to the reforming ambitions of social democratic parties. The former produced an organizational model of socialism as an authoritarian state bureaucracy rooted in a single party, a model that was to be imposed in some places and adopted in others where socialism presented itself as an agency for nation building and economic development. The latter produced an organizational model of socialism rooted in the increasingly bureaucratized social democratic parties (the oligarchic character of which had been identified early in the century with reference to the German party by Michels in his *Political Parties*), whose central activity has been to press more functions and responsibilities upon an expanding state in the cause of economic and social welfare, but without giving much thought to the consequences of this activity in terms of the organization of an enlarged state or wider socialist objectives.

If these are arguments from practice relevant to the development of socialist statism, there are also of course some important arguments from theory. As was seen earlier, there is a major tradition of organizational socialism, the main thrust of which is to indict capitalism for the waste and inefficiency consequent upon the anarchy of competition and to counterpose this with the merits of socialist planning. It is clear that the planning argument encompasses a number of themes basic to the socialist position, and equally clear that it is an argument that carries with it a strong centralist bias and an antipathy to a diversity of economic and social initiatives. In his *Farewell to the Working Class*, André Gorz makes this point well:

The source of the theoretical superiority of socialism over capitalism is thus the source of its practical inferiority. To argue that society should be the controlled, programmed result of its members' activity is to demand that everyone should make their conduct functional to the overall social result in view. Thus, there can be no room for any form of conduct which, if generalised, would not lead to the programmed social outcome. Classical socialist doctrine finds it difficult to come to terms with political and social pluralism, understood not simply as a plurality of parties and trade unions but as the coexistence of various ways of working, producing and living, various and distinct cultural areas and levels of social existence.

So, too, with the commitment to equality, which has naturally nourished a centralist politics of collective provision and uniform administration. The modern administrative state has emerged out of this process in which national provision has increasingly replaced local provision, voluntarism has been displaced by professionalization, and uniformity imposed on an untidy diversity. It need hardly be said that this process has brought with it many real achievements (though perhaps it does need to be said that bureaucracies have considerable merits), but it has also involved a number of other consequences for socialism. It has been accompanied by the atrophy of the myriad forms of working-class self-help and democracy, as attention has become increasingly focused on the legislative possibilities of central state power. Thus A. H. Halsey describes the process whereby, in Britain, 'the Labour movement set out to nationalise democracy and welfare, to translate fraternity, equality and liberty from the local community to the national state' and in doing so was 'ironically fated to develop through its political party the threats of a bureaucratic state'.

From a number of directions, therefore, it is possible to chart the development of a socialist statism, at the expense of alternative socialist traditions. However, in order to get these matters into clearer focus, it is necessary to say something about their place in traditional socialist thought. In some ways what is of most significance is how little space has in fact been occupied by serious discussion of structural and constitutional aspects of socialism, either in terms of the organization of a socialist economy or of a socialist political system. Such preoccupations were part of the hallmark of the 'utopianism' from which Marx wanted to distance his own scientific socialism. It is well known that Marx was consistently dismissive of those who raised questions about the future organization of a socialist society, a futile pastime that was like writing 'recipes for the cookshops of the future'. The organization of future society would necessarily be a matter for those involved in making it.

This approach came to characterize the classical Marxist tradition. Thus Kautsky explained in *The Class Struggle* (1892) that concern with the structure of the future social order was 'wholly irreconcilable with the point of view of modern science', since it would be the determined product of the process of economic development that gave rise to it; so 'few things are, therefore, more childish than to demand of the socialist that he draw a picture of the commonwealth which he strives for'. If this seems sensible enough, consider also some of its assumptions and implications. It involves a refusal to think through the structural principles of socialist society, not merely its organizational details. The assumption is that there is only a single structural principle that matters, the replacement of private property by public property in the means of production, and that all else may be derived through practice from that.

This did not, of course, prevent Marx from describing the comprehensive transformation in the human condition that would flow from this single structural change. It inaugurates a realm of freedom, of unalienated creativity consequent upon the abolition of the division of labour, when it becomes 'possible for me to do one thing today and another tomorrow, to hunt in the morning, fish in the afternoon, rear cattle in the evening, criticise after dinner, just as I have a mind, without ever becoming hunter, fisherman, cowherd, or critic'. In citing this memorable formulation here the purpose is not to explore some of the familiar objections to it (for example, the technocratic objection—how does it apply to brain surgeons and airline pilots?) or the feminist objection (who does the cooking and washes the dishes?), but to identify a mode of thought in which it is possible to leap from an initial structural change to its most audacious consequences *with nothing else in between*. Indeed, attempts to clarify the character of this middle ground are likely to be dismissed as unscientific and unhistorical.

Thus Marx offers an extended analysis of the political economy of capitalism, but nothing similar for socialism. It is enough, it seems, that socialism is non-capitalism. In *Capital* there is reference to a socialist economy in terms of 'production by freely associated men . . . consciously regulated by them in accordance with a settled plan', but this is not thought to require any further consideration of the terms on which free association, conscious regulation, and settled plan might need to be reconciled as the basis for a workable, non-coercive socialist economy. It is not that Marx should have produced, in addition to his other prodigious labours, a working model of a socialist economy, but that his approach evidenced no recognition that a socialist economy would still be an arena of scarcity, choice, conflict, and decision. Such a recognition might seem important in itself, but it becomes even more important in view of the marked centralist bias in Marxist economic thought and its disparagement of the small-scale and particular. It is the centralizing, concentrationist thrust of capitalism that provides the necessary preconditions for socialism, replacing small production in industry and agriculture and needing only to be socialized to become the unitary economy of socialist rationality. As Kautsky once put it, socialist society was therefore to be seen as 'nothing more than a single gigantic industrial concern'.

In view of this, the question of how a wholly centralized socialist economy was to be run, and by whom, might seem to be of more than passing interest. In *The Economics of Feasible Socialism*, Alec Nove points attention (from his perspective as a leading authority on the planned economies of Eastern Europe) to 'the fact that the functional logic of centralised planning "fits" far too easily into the practice of centralised despotism'. While there is no difficulty in showing that Marx was a radical democrat and republican apostle of liberty, it is also the case that he originated a mode of analysis which made it impossible to consider the problems raised by a possible 'fit' of this kind. It was the anarchist Bakunin who first pressed the question of how a centralized economy could be reconciled with political liberty, and it was a question to which Marx provided no adequate answer. Bakunin's own answer (which became the standard charge against Marxists from anarchists and syndicalists) was to point towards the creation of a new kind of state despotism by the 'scientific' socialists:

The terms 'scientific socialist' and 'scientific socialism', which we meet incessantly in the works and speeches of the Lassallists and Marxists, are sufficient to prove that the so-called people's state will be nothing but a despotism over the masses, exercised by a new and quite small aristocracy of real or bogus 'scientists'. The people, being unlearned, will be completely exempted from the task of governing and will be forced into the herd of those who are governed. A fine sort of emancipation!

It is not enough, then, simply to acquit Marx of any despotic propensities, if at the same time it can be shown that his analysis left too many hostages to fortune. Bakunin's point is a real one, and it has gained added weight from the experience of postrevolutionary socialist societies in the twentieth century, in which the authority of Marxist 'science' has buttressed the power of ruling Marxist parties to produce the sort of despotic consequences with which the world has become all too familiar. It is scarcely adequate to claim that such consequences have nothing to do with classical Marxism (an inadequacy that does not, of course, prevent the claim being made) when it is evident that classical Marxism has refused to take seriously the whole question of socialist democracy, secure in the knowledge that the 'associated producers' will ensure that everything works out all right on the night. 'If Marxist political theory is to learn how to realise its own emancipatory project', writes John Dunn (in his *Western Political Theory in the Face of the Future*), 'it needs to develop a quite new level and style of reflection on the question of how in practice and in principle the battle of democracy could be won.'

This directs attention to Marxist political theory itself, the real centre of this whole discussion. Marx's inadequate treatment of the structural principles of socialism is a reflection of a theoretical position that deals inadequately with politics in general, reducing it to a subordinate and derivative status. There is no systematic political theorizing to be found in classical Marxism, for (as Miliband puts it in his *Marxism and Politics*) 'the available classical writings are simply silent or extremely perfunctory over major issues of politics and political theory'. Thus the absence of any sustained analysis of the state by Marx is matched by an equivalent neglect of the organizational problems of socialism. Those in search of Marx's understanding of the character of the provisional 'revolutionary dictatorship of the proletariat' or of the subsequent 'abolition of all classes' have to rummage amongst a scatter of often inconsistent references and usages. While this provides much harmless diversion for the constantly replenished army of Marx exegetes, it also emphasizes the gap where a coherent political analysis should be.

This gap was filled, at least with respect to political organization, only by Marx's assorted references to the necessity of a temporary (though also 'energetic') period of proletarian dictatorship, to be followed by a stateless communism in which 'there will be no more political power properly so-called'. The character of the revolutionary exercise of power by the proletariat as envisaged by Marx remains a source of dispute. On the

one hand, it is presented in terms of an intensification of centralized state power in the hands of the proletariat, as in his 1850
March Address, where Marx declared that 'the task of the really
revolutionary party [is] to carry through the strictest centralisation'. On the other hand, though, in his discussion of the 1871
Paris Commune in *The Civil War in France*, Marx eulogized the
decentralized democracy of the Commune that had been constructed on the smashed ruins of the existing state as 'the political
form at last discovered under which to work out the economic
emancipation of labour'. It represented Marx's belief that socialism would be distinguished, in David McLellan's phrase, by
the 'deprofessionalisation of governmental functions'. Marx
described what this meant in terms of the Commune:

The majority of its members were naturally working men, or acknowledged representatives of the working class. The Commune was to be a
working not a parliamentary body, executive and legislative at the same
time. Instead of continuing to be the agent of the Central Government,
the police was at once stripped of its political attributes, and turned into
the responsible and at all times revocable agent of the Commune. So
were the officials of all other branches of the Administration. From the
members of the Commune downwards, the public service had to be done
at workmen's wages . . . Public functions ceased to be the private property of the tools of the Central Government. Not only municipal
administration, but the whole initiative hitherto exercised by the state
was laid into the hands of the Commune.

But did the Commune structure also represent, contrary to
what Marx had seemed to suggest previously, the dictatorship of
the proletariat (as Engels was later to declare), or was it to be seen
as an anticipation of the durable political structure of a socialist
society, even though the Commune itself was 'merely the rising of
a city under exceptional circumstances' as Marx subsequently
described it? What is significant is that this matter has to be left in
the form of a question. Nowhere does Marx provide an answer to
the key questions concerning the organization of the proletarian
dictatorship, such as the terms on which central political power
will connect with a decentralized commune structure and, in
Bakunin's question, the sense in which the proletariat 'as a
whole' would be in government.

What is even more significant is that nowhere in classical
Marxism is there a developed account of a socialist political

system that confronts the basic questions to be asked of any political system. These are questions concerning the nature of representation and accountability, the organization of political competition and opposition, the methods by which conflicts are resolved, and the forms of political liberty. The reasons for this neglect are not difficult to locate. They spring from the derivative status of politics in the Marxist tradition, reflected in the belief that the state and the whole apparatus of 'bourgeois' political life is an expression of the class antagonism of capitalism and therefore destined to disappear when socialism abolishes the cause of social antagonism. In Marx's words, 'there will be no more political power properly so-called'. A unitary society, without classes, would not require the political machinery needed by a divided society. In practice, of course, this has been converted into the rule of the single party in the name of the single class, sustained by the definitional denial that any grounds for political division and opposition can exist. Nor can this be dismissed as an illegitimate conversion, when it derives from a theoretical tradition that identifies political (and other) antagonisms as essentially a derivation from class antagonisms. The twentieth-century party-state has finally buried this model of political dependency (or should have done), even though itself constructed out of the theoretical tradition that produced it.

It is not sufficient, therefore, to register the fact that the classical Marxist tradition neglects to offer a developed account of the organizational structure of socialism, unless it is also understood that such neglect is not an oversight but an authentic expression of its central assumptions. The only structural change that mattered was in property relations, from which all else would flow, in ways that could not be anticipated by utopian speculation, but would be determined by the historical actors themselves. However, socialism's abolition of the class antagonism that sustained the political machinery of capitalism was the guarantee of an integrated democracy under socialism, the reflection of a unitary society. There could be no more comprehensive guarantee than this, requiring no elaborate small print. It promised, quite literally, an end to politics. Some kind of 'public power' would remain, but there was no need to quibble about the simple administrative forms that this would take.

The promise has been fulfilled, though scarcely in the form

intended. Those regimes that have transmuted this mode of thought into their official ideology have indeed delivered an end to politics, or at least the closest approximation to it that the world has yet seen. The crucial, poignant, figure in this process is Lenin. It was Lenin who, in his *State and Revolution*, written on the eve of the Bolshevik revolution, translated the general conception of an end to politics into an account of the structure of popular self-administration that would replace the state in post-revolutionary society. It was also Lenin who, in the wake of the revolution, presided over the development of an authoritarianism rooted in the 'democratic centralism' of a single party and a repressive state bureaucracy. There is no need to resort to a cynical explanation to account for this shift. The former represented Lenin's solution in terms of Marxist *theory* to the question of post-revolutionary organization; while the latter represented his solution in *practice*. Only those attached to a particular view of the unity of theory and practice need be surprised by such a disjuncture.

Something was said earlier about Lenin's need, contrary to the familiar view of him as a revolutionary opportunist, to ground his political practice in a secure basis of Marxist theory. If this was true of his account of the conditions which made revolution possible, it was also true of his account of post-revolutionary society. He satisfied himself, following Bukharin, that a Marxist revolution would need to destroy the existing state machine and, following Marx, that it would be replaced by a system of popular self-government on the Commune model. Thus it was Lenin, in his *State and Revolution*, who (as Harding puts it) 'rescued the commune from oblivion'. He argued that Marx's description of the Commune had established the correct form of socialist organization; that the soviets were the practical embodiment of this form; and that capitalist imperialism had developed the processes of production and distribution to an organizational point at which they could be run on simplified lines by a system of popular self-administration.

What this would mean was confidently described by Lenin in this familiar passage:

We the workers, shall organize large-scale production on the basis of what capitalism has already created, relying on our own experience as workers, establishing strict, iron discipline backed up by the state power of the armed workers. We shall reduce the role of state officials to that of simply carrying out our instructions as responsible, revocable, modestly paid 'foremen and accountants' . . . This is our proletarian task, this is what we can and must start with in accomplishing the proletarian revolution. Such a beginning, on the basis of large-scale production, will of itself lead to the gradual 'withering away' of all bureaucracy, to the gradual creation of an order . . . under which the functions of control and accounting, becoming more and more simple, will be performed by each in turn, will then become a habit and will finally die out as the *special* functions of a special section of the population.

This account of a decentralized, participatory democracy under socialism (in which 'all will govern in turn and will soon become accustomed to no one governing') represents the culmination of a tradition. It is the fulfilment of Marx's original Promethean, emancipatory vision of active self-government, the final realization of the classical democratic ideal itself.

However, as the culmination of a tradition it is also the place (as A. J. Polan has argued to such good effect in his *Lenin and the End of Politics*) where the flaws in that tradition stand out in sharpest relief. There is the underlying assumption that political and administrative consequences can simply be read off from an analysis of economic development. There is the repudiation of 'bourgeois' politics that takes literally the idea that, under socialism, the government of men is replaced by the administration of things. There is the assumption that the social unity represented by socialism means that there can be no legitimate grounds for organized disunity. Thus Lenin reflects a tradition that offers democracy without division, administration without politics, civic activity without civil liberty. Behind the lyrical account of a self-managing society, there lurks the 'state power of the armed workers', while the absence of any discussion of the party in *State and Revolution* (confined to a single, fleeting reference) simply served to identify the political vacuum that it was destined to fill. Lenin's earlier *What is to be done?* was to prove a more reliable guide to the organizational imperatives of socialist revolution.

It is difficult to overstate the significance of Leninism, in this respect as in others, and of what may be called the Leninist moment in the development of socialist forms. Established positions and traditional assumptions were thrown into confusion.

Classical Marxism, certainly as represented by the Second
International theorists, had assumed that socialism would extend
existing democratic forms, not negate them. Thus Kautsky was
quick to denounce the political despotism of Bolshevism, but this
denunciation also served to expose how unexplored had been the
political assumptions of the Marxist tradition. Perhaps the most
telling critique of Bolshevik political repression from within the
Marxist tradition came from Rosa Luxemburg, not on the sort of
general liberal grounds advanced by Kautsky but on the grounds
that political dictatorship by the party prevented the free development of the class. The revolution required political freedom
and democracy if it was not to atrophy: 'Without general elec-
tions, without unrestricted freedom of press and assembly, without a free struggle of opinion, life dies out in every public
institution, becomes a mere semblance of life, in which only the
bureaucracy remains as the active element.' However, Luxemburg's point could be put rather differently: Bolshevism had
demonstrated that it was an illusion to suppose that socialist
revolution would necessarily take a democratic, libertarian form
and that despotic, bureaucratic forms were also available (and,
perhaps, more likely).

Such matters did not present themselves so clearly to most
socialists in the immediate aftermath of the Bolshevik revolution,
or in the turbulent period that followed the end of the First World
War. It was possible to regard the soviets as the concrete form of
direct democracy under socialism, the solution in socialist terms
to the question of political organization. Thus in Italy in
1918–20, Gramsci could present the Turin workers-council
movement as part of this same 'council' conception of socialist
democracy, in opposition to rule by party, parliament, or
bureaucracy. It was a form of power that came from below, not
imposed from the top, and the organizational structure of socialist society was to be seen in terms of a network of relationships
between working-class institutions: 'To link these institutions,
coordinating and ordering them into a highly centralised hierar-
chy of competencies and powers, while respecting the necessary
autonomy and articulation of each, is to create a genuine workers'
democracy here and now—a workers' democracy in effective and
active opposition to the bourgeois State, and prepared to replace
it here and now in all its essential functions of administering
and controlling the national heritage.'

This 'conciliar' communism was destined to become a minority tradition following the collapse of the post-war working-class militancy (its continued advocacy in the inter-war years being associated with such forgotten figures as the Dutch anti-Bolshevik Pannekoek). Much of it was simply swallowed up in Lenin's organization of an international communism to wrest the leadership of the Western working class from reformist social democracy. Even those who, in significant senses, were not Leninists were forced in this polarization to range themselves on the side of 'revolution' against 'reform'. This involved, as with Gramsci, a shift of emphasis from council to party as the organizational model. It also involved a belief on the part of many anti-authoritarian revolutionaries that 'after the revolution', or more accurately after the period of discipline and dictatorship necessary to consolidate the revolution, then the way would be clear for the establishment of a self-governing society of the kind outlined in Lenin's *State and Revolution*. For example, the syndicalist Tom Mann could declare that 'the outlook for the future is not that of a centralised official bureaucracy giving instructions and commands to servile subordinates (but) . . . the coming of associations of equals'; but could then go on to affirm his support for the Third International because 'with the experience of Russia to guide us, I entirely agree that there will be a period, short or long, when the dictatorship of the proletariat must be resorted to'. Even at the time this was written, the soviets were being subsumed by party and state. Soon there would be everything from 'Soviet' power to 'Soviet' circuses; but the only thing there would not be were the soviets.

If the organized split within international socialism had the effect, reinforced by the slackening of the post-war working-class militancy, that by the early 1920s the libertarian and self-managing strands of Marxism had been effectively buried by an authoritarian communism, then a similar process had occurred on the other side of the socialist divide. In Britain, for example, the Fabians had developed a collectivist doctrine that represented an administrative version of socialism. In his contribution to *Fabian Essays*, Bernard Shaw explained 'the distinctive term Social Democrat' as 'indicating the man or woman who desires through Democracy to gather the whole people into the State, so that the State may be trusted with the rent of the country, and finally with the land, the capital, and the organisation of the national industry—with all the sources of production, in short, which are now abandoned to the cupidity of irresponsible private individuals'. It should, perhaps, be said that the early Fabians were not quite the rigid state centralists as often described, not least because of the municipal emphasis that envisaged a major role for the local state. Nor should the historical reputation of Fabianism be allowed to obscure the fact that other strands in early British socialism were associational rather than organizational, reflected in Keir Hardie's ethical socialism that expected a period of statism to be merely the necessary preliminary to a mutualist communism or, more significantly, in William Morris's powerful rejection of state socialism in both its revolutionary or reformist versions and consistent advocacy of an associational socialism of decentralized self-government.

However, when these qualifications are entered, it remains the case that classical Fabianism represented a particular kind of socialism. It was a collectivist kind that emphasized the organizational attributes of socialism in arranging efficient production and egalitarian distribution through its control of the national and local state. It also set its face against other kinds of socialism, not merely against revolutionary socialism, but against all those kinds of socialism in which self-government (usually of producers) was the central emphasis. This gives a particular interest to the period, roughly the second decade of this century, when Fabian collectivism was challenged by the ideas of the guild socialists (at a time when industrial militancy had raised demands for workers' control, and when the sovereignty of the state was under intellectual challenge from the pluralists). The guild socialists, with G. D. H. Cole as their leading figure, argued that socialism was about freedom and self-government, crucially in the work-place but extending throughout society; and looked forward to the development of the trade unions from their present negative, defensive role into self-governing industrial guilds responsible for the control of industry and forming the nucleus of a guild society.

Guild socialism claimed to be a synthesis of syndicalism and collectivism. The former was right in its emphasis on the centrality of industrial freedom, but was flawed by a sectionalism that failed to acknowledge a general interest that included the interests of consumers. The latter avoided the central defect of syndicalism but also its crucial merit. The elaborate system building of the guild socialists was designed to construct a workable synthesis between these positions. If the infirmities and dangers of collectivism were particularly emphasized, it was because they represented a future that was already immanent in the present. In his *Self Government in Industry* (1917), Cole noted how 'today we are moving at a headlong pace in the direction of a ''national'' control of the lives of men'; and how 'in the State of today, in which democratic control through Parliament is little better than a farce, the Collectivist State would be the Earthly Paradise of bureaucracy'. It might offer more security, but it would not change the subordinate status of the workers nor offer more general scope for the exercise of freedom and democracy. Because of this, it would not effect any significant change in human motivation, and would not prove to be a kind of socialism capable of producing a popular response on a durable basis.

Like the 'council' movement within Marxism, guild socialism was destined to fade from view in the early 1920s, another victim of the great divide. Yet for a time it had seemed that guild socialist and associated ideas had opened up an alternative direction for socialism in Britain. There had taken place a period of sustained debate over several years on the structural form of socialism, combining political theory and practical example. This debate had addressed such key issues as the balance between producer and consumer interests, democracy and efficiency, territorial and functional devolution. In 1920 both Cole (in his *Guild Socialism Restated*) and the Webbs (in their *Constitution for the Socialist Commonwealth of Great Britain*) offered their developed thoughts on the structural form of socialism. If their emphasis remained different, both positions reflected a prevailing belief that it was important to think through the structural form of the distribution of power under socialism (and that such matters could not simply be left until, and resolved by, the coming of socialism). The socialist basis adopted by the Labour Party in 1918, with its coupling of 'common ownership' and 'popular administration', reflected this prevailing climate of ideas.

Yet this opening towards a decentralized, self-managing version of socialism was to be effectively sealed off for the next half century. It found no place in the organized antagonism between communists and social democrats. The former had adopted a model of party authoritarianism, while the latter had settled for a cautious reformism that involved protestations of faith in existing constitutional arrangements. Economic depression took its toll of the labour movement's energy and imagination, and turned eyes towards the state as the means of redress. The widespread attraction of the idea of economic planning (influenced by the Russian example) served to strengthen the emphasis on state centralism. The dark shadows cast by fascism and Stalinism could be interpreted in terms of the need to be wary of new political forms and to settle for established ones. This is historical shorthand, of course, but the effects of these assorted influences were evident in a political practice that was increasingly deaf to the distant voices of a socialist pluralism. In Britain, for example, socialization became nationalization and in the bureaucratic form of the public corporation that denied the claims of producer democracy; while the 1945 Labour Government can now be seen to have been 'sternly centralist' (K. O. Morgan, *Labour in Power 1945–1951*), despite the former guild socialist sympathies of its prime minister.

In one significant respect, however, this story can be told less negatively. The political experiences of this century at least provided the materials out of which could be constructed a 'democratic socialism' with an identity sharply different from its authoritarian form (although the fact that so many socialists in the West fudged this task for so long is also part of the history of our times). No longer could it be supposed that the conversion of private into public ownership of the means of production was sufficient to make redundant any concern with the political organization of freedom. R. H. Tawney made the essential point: 'The truth is that a conception of Socialism which views it as involving the nationalization of everything except political power, on which all else depends, is not, to speak with moderation, according to light. The question is not merely whether the State owns and controls the means of production. It is also who owns and controls the State.'

Moreover, this question could be regarded as more, not less, important for socialists to tackle in so far as socialism would augment the general power of the state by adding economic power to political power. This last point had been emphasized earlier by Jaurès, in presenting socialism (in his *Socialist Organisation*) in terms of a diversification of economic power and decentralization of political power: 'If the politicians and administrators who already control the nation's diplomacy and armed forces were also given authority over the whole labour force, and if they could appoint managers at all levels in the same way as they now appoint army officers, this would confer on a handful of men such power as Asian despots never dreamt of— for they controlled only the surface of public life and not the economy of their countries.' It became important, therefore, for democratic socialists to identify their kind of socialism as involving civil and political liberty and effective mechanisms for political representation and accountability. It would incorporate and extend the democratic freedoms won under capitalism, not abrogate them in the name of an illusory conception of 'socialist' freedom.

However, the construction of a democratic socialist position of this kind confronted a number of difficulties. It was undermined by a communist version of Marxism which propagated the view, most successfully in the 'red decade' of the 1930s, that the whole apparatus of 'capitalist' freedom and democracy was essentially bogus because of its class character. However, it also faced dilution from a version of social democracy that responded to its loss of theoretical and political confidence by slackening its attachment to socialism in its firm embrace of existing constitutional arrangements. The twentieth century had made it harder, if more necessary, to link socialism and democracy; and harder still to argue for a democratic socialism that did not merely affirm the compatability of socialism and parliamentary democracy but went beyond this to offer a kind of socialism which had democracy as its active, organizing principle.

But was there, and is there, an available democratic socialism of this kind? Or is it the case, as critics of socialism have long argued, that the organizational imperatives of socialism can lead only (at best) to bureaucratic rule and (at worst) to something even more tyrannical? 'I for one cannot visualise', wrote Schumpeter, 'in the conditions of modern society, a socialist organization in any form other than that of a huge and all-embracing bureaucratic apparatus.' Such questions could, perhaps, be avoided by socialists when they remained at the level of theory; but during this century they have become urgent questions from the world of political practice. Even where a self-managing socialism has been established, as in Yugoslavia, the maintenance of the dominant political role of the party prevents it being taken as evidence of the combination of socialism and democracy. The evidence that it was quite possible for them *not* to be combined, and the lack of evidence of a more positive kind, has had a profound influence on socialist thinking (and on thinking about socialism). In the 1940s, reviewing Hayek's *The Road to Serfdom*, George Orwell summed up 'our present predicament' in these terms: 'Capitalism leads to dole queues, the scramble for markets, and war. Collectivism leads to concentration camps, leader worship and war. There is no way out of this unless a planned economy can somehow be combined with the freedom of the intellect . . .'

Orwell went on to register the depressing fact that nobody seemed able to translate this 'somehow' into a practical programme. If this sounded like the voice of the mid-century reaction to Stalinism, the democratic socialist predicament could still be expressed in remarkably similar terms two decades later. In *The Long Revolution*, Raymond Williams described the deadlock in thinking about social change that stemmed from the fact that 'we seem reduced to a choice between speculator and bureaucrat, and while we do not like the speculators, the bureaucrat is not exactly inviting either. In such a situation, energy is sapped, hope weakens, and of course the present compromise between the speculators and the bureaucrats remains unchallenged.' An authoritarian model of socialism was on offer from the communists, while social democratic collectivism seemed able only to offer the prospect of an enlarged state bureaucracy as the organizational model of a welfare capitalism. If this prospect caused some socialist voices to be raised in resistance (for example, in the post-war *New Fabian Essays* Richard Crossman argued that 'the planned economy and the centralisation of power are no longer socialist objectives'), for a long time these remained minority voices and their effect was to reinforce the retreat from socialism rather than to promote its democratic restatement.

However, in this respect as in others, the loosening of the rival

socialist blocs in the 1950s and 1960s has produced its consequences. An independent Marxism has been able to undertake its
own critique of the Soviet state, turning from Leninism to
Gramsci and reclaiming a tradition of 'council' communism, and
endeavouring to restate the emancipatory promise of original
Marxism in terms capable of carrying conviction in the late-
twentieth-century world. The cultural revolution in the West in
the 1960s found its political expression (most conspicuously in
the *événéments* of 1968) in a rejection of the bureaucratic character of both organized communism and organized social democracy, and in a reassertion of libertarian, self-managing traditions
(not always, it might be added, in very libertarian ways). A
central aspect of Eurocommunism has involved the acknowledgement of the validity of the Western model of political democracy; while in the socialist parties of Europe there has been a
renewed interest in producer democracy and the democratic diffusion of power. In France, for example, 'autogestion' was a key
ideological element in the revival of French socialism in the
1970s. During the same period Swedish socialism (partly in
response to the offensive from radical liberalism) reformulated
its doctrinal basis to emphasize the role of producer democracy in
the general extension of democracy that was now identified as the
distinctive project of democratic socialism. In Germany, too,
part of the process of reversing the deradicalization of German
socialism that had culminated in the 1959 Bad Godesberg programme turned on the need for a democratic, non-bureaucratic
socialism in which 'basis groups' would share power with the
state. The Bad Godesberg programme had contained the famous
formulation: 'competition as far as possible, planning as far
as necessary'. In 1974 this could be nicely reformulated (by
the left-wing Social Democrat, Strasser): 'As much autogestion
as possible, as much central planning and administration as
necessary'.

   More generally, some of the most innovative recent socialist
thought in Europe (for example, the work of Gorz and Bahro)
has been concerned to argue the case for the contemporary rel-
evance of an autonomist, decentralized version of socialism and
the irrelevance of organizational, productionist versions. The
technological arguments that were formerly deployed against a
small-scale, self-managing socialism could now be stood on their

head. However, there are considerable difficulties involved in translating new theoretical perspectives into a viable socialist project, not least because of the continuing strength of socialist traditions that point in different directions. Bureaucratic collectivism remains a powerful element within both the communist and social democratic movements in the West. Moreover, the attempts to escape from this through various forms of anti-politics (whether benign or malign, personal or collective) have to be regarded as flights of fancy that are testimony to the contemporary dilemmas of socialism rather than contributions to their resolution.

It seems reasonably clear that a democratic socialism seriously committed *both* to socialism *and* democracy and seeking to present socialism in essentially democratic terms would need to have theorized a structure that would make this possible. In political terms, this would require an attention to the constitutional structure of a socialist society, in which the state would continue to exist as the major focus for allocation decisions and would need to be securely rooted in a developed structure of political representation, political competition, and political and civic freedom. In other words, a political structure in which there is more democracy, not less. In economic terms, it would require (as Alec Nove has argued in *The Economics of Feasible Socialism*) an economic structure in which the predominance of social ownership takes a diversity of forms, there is a preference for the small scale and the self-managing, central economic planning is confined to major strategic decisions, market choice and competition still operate subject to certain ground rules, and some material inequality is accepted as necessary for a free labour market but is consciously limited. In other words, an economic structure in which there is plan and market, centralism and decentralization, state control and producer democracy. A democratic socialism of this kind would be one in which democracy does not stop at the factory gate, nor at the factory exit. However, it would also be a kind of socialism which has been a minority tradition for much of socialism's history.

6. Actors

The crisis of socialism is above all a reflection of the crisis of the proletariat.

André Gorz

If socialism is to come, who is to bring it about? Who are its actors and agents? In terms of the general line of argument being pursued here, such familiar questions require a further refinement: what kinds of actors are envisaged and embraced by what kinds of socialism? For a long time it seemed that socialists had a secure, unproblematical answer to this central question of agency, with any difficulties confined to the margin. At the end of the twentieth century this is manifestly no longer the case. If it is now possible for a socialist like André Gorz to wave a convincing *Farewell to the Working Class*, it is much less clear to whom socialists are now waving a convincing greeting.

Why has this matter of agency moved to the centre of socialist discussion? Why has an axiom (the working class as the carrier of socialism) turned into a question? A number of issues are clearly involved here, but perhaps two in particular should be identified at once because of their central importance. At this stage they are only sketched out, to be returned to later. Firstly, there is the extent to which, in socialist political practice, the movement of a class has been converted into the organization of a party. The working class as socialist actor has been supplemented by the party as the agent of the class. At one level, this may be said merely to have raised necessary questions about the relationship of class to party. At another level, however, it has opened up the whole question of 'substitutism', the extent to which the party has not just supplemented class action but substituted itself for it. Moreover, as Trotsky had warned in 1904, this process could be carried further: 'the party organisation at first substitutes itself for the party as a whole; then the central committee substitutes itself for the organisation; and finally a single "dictator" substitutes himself for the central committee.' For obvious reasons, this process of substitution has been seen as having a particular application to the twentieth-century communist tradition. However, it should also be noted that similar lines of analysis have been pursued in relation to the social democratic parties.

The second main reason for the contemporary preoccupation with the matter of socialist agency may be stated even more bluntly. Socialism's traditional actors have not displayed a reliable talent for keeping to their script. Not only do they frequently get their lines wrong, but sometimes even seem to think they are taking part in a different production. The Western working class has not merely failed to fulfil the revolutionary role assigned to it by classical Marxism (a role last glimpsed in the second decade of this century), but has seemed to become ever *less* revolutionary. Lenin's fears after 1914 that the Western working class, unless given decisive revolutionary leadership, would be incorporated into 'bourgeois reformism' through the treacherous agency of the social democrats would seem to have been amply vindicated. However, even in reformist terms, working-class support for social democracy has not generally been sufficient to secure the durable reconstruction of these societies on a social democratic basis. The experience of fascism (an experience that included the fact that over 30 per cent of Nazi Party members were manual workers, part of a class that had been regarded as the most promising socialist material in Europe) opened up the prospect of a mass mobilization of the Right and dented (in some cases, even inverted) traditional socialist expectations. In recent decades the changing character of class structures in the West has been identified as presenting new questions concerning the political role of the working class, and of socialist agency in general; while outside the West such questions have been asked and answered in ways that have introduced socialist actors of new kinds in unfamiliar roles.

Against this sort of background, it is scarcely surprising then that the matter of socialist agency has acquired considerable significance today. In the 1840s Marx dismissed and derided the 'utopian' socialists on this same ground. The absence of any convincing agency in their schemes was a reflection of the unhistorical and unscientific character of their general approach, and constituted the basis of their utopianism. Thus Saint-Simon presented his 'system' to successive regimes in France and in particular to a motley assortment of groups (*les industriels*) who would reorganize society on a new productionist basis; meanwhile Fourier sat around waiting for the patron who would fund the social experiments that would vindicate his schemes and save the world from its misery. It was against such utopianism that the young Marx directed his materialist account of the motor of historical development. As the famous opening words of the *Communist Manifesto* announced it: 'The history of all hitherto existing society is the history of class struggles.'

When translated into the present, what this meant was that socialists did not have to cast around for a suitable agency for the socialist project but merely recognize that both the project and its agent were immanent in the historical process itself. What was required was an initial act of recognition, not of invention. Capitalism was the contemporary form of the class appropriation of the means of production but, like previous appropriations, it had generated its own internal forces of antagonism and eventual transcendence. These forces were represented by the proletariat, the creation of capitalism but also its antagonist and revolutionary successor. The proletariat would develop in size, strength, organization, and consciousness as capitalism itself developed. In this process it would develop from a class *in* itself to a class *for* itself. A progressive simplification of class forces was underway, as intermediate, petty-bourgeois elements were swallowed up by the class polarization into the 'two great hostile camps' of bourgeoisie and proletariat. The hostility would reach its 'decisive hour' in conditions of capitalist crisis and proletarian pauperization, when the proletariat would emancipate itself through a revolution of the 'immense majority' and thereby also deliver humanity from the final form of class oppression and antagonism. 'What the bourgeoisie therefore, produces, above all, is its own gravediggers. Its fall and the victory of the proletariat are equally inevitable.'

So here was the installation of the working class as the revolutionary subject, the carrier of socialism. If the sketch given here is in the dramatic idiom of the *Manifesto*, needing to be filled out and qualified in various respects to take account of later positions, it does nevertheless represent the essential Marxist perspective. Socialism was to be achieved through the revolutionary action of the working class; indeed, socialism *was* the revolutionary victory of the working class. There could be no question of whether class struggle was desirable or undesirable, since it was the essential fact about social and economic life under capitalism. It conditioned everything else, and was destined to end in a particular kind of resolution. It was reflected in the various forms of struggle of labour against capital, and in the developing industrial and political organization of the forces of labour. There might be room for argument and adjustment about the precise moment and conditions in which the proletariat would come to power, but that it would come to power was as certain as night followed day. It did not matter either that Marx had offered no sustained account of the nature of social class, since classes defined themselves in terms of their relationship to the means of production and revealed themselves through action.

Before turning to some of the issues that have been associated with this identification of the revolutionary subject by Marx, something should be said about the nature of the identification itself. It is an indication of the severity of the contemporary crisis in socialist thought on the matter of agency that, even from within the Marxist tradition, voices are to be heard asking not only the now familiar questions about the relationship between class position and class behaviour but beyond this to the fundamental question concerning the identification of the revolutionary subject itself. Put simply, what if Marx got it wrong? This question is now framed not just in terms of the evident gap between the prospectus and the performance, but in terms that cast doubt on the basis of the original identification. As Rudolf Bahro has written: 'It might well have been no more than a Hegelian error to have burdened a particular class, and a class restricted by its position in the reproduction process, with the fate of humanity as a whole.'

In other words, the world-historic mission of the proletariat begins to look like a philosophical invention on Marx's part. It was the product of a position that held that—to paraphrase the words of *The Holy Family* quoted earlier—what mattered was what the proletariat essentially *was* and, because of what it was, what it would necessarily *do*. Its historical role was assigned to it without an audition. Nor did it matter that its performance in the leading historical role might cast doubt on its ability as an actor, or might even suggest that it was unaware of what its role actually was, since it would necessarily 'become what it is'. For Marx, then, it was not observation of the proletariat in action that provided the basis for his casting (nor his own limited engagement with working-class political activity), but initially and primarily it was the product of a process of philosophical reflection. This extended into, and was sustained by, a view of capitalist development as involving a homogenizing proletarianization of labour carried to a point at which a class of collective labourers having nothing to lose but their chains has both the capacity and the necessity to free itself through an act of collective appropriation. However, this account of proletarianization was again not the product of historical analysis but a working out of what the proletariat would have to become and do because of what, in *essence*, it was. This point is well made by Gorz:

Marx described the process of proletarianisation in such a way as to show that it would produce a proletariat conscious of its being, that is to say, forced by vital necessity to become what it is to be. The historical analysis was so weak, however, that it was incapable of factually supporting the thesis it was designed to underpin. At his conclusion, Marx had returned to his point of departure and had failed to develop an analysis which substantially enriched his initial intuition.

It would, of course, be absurd to conclude from this that socialism had acquired an agency simply through a process of philosophical invention on Marx's part. It was plausible to believe that the class of wage labourers that had been brought into existence by capitalism, and that was the victim of the systematic exploitation revealed by Marx's analysis of the operation of the capitalist economy, would also be the class that would provide the opposition to capitalism. It was this class, the working class, that had a direct *interest* in opposing capitalism. This interest was reflected in the development of industrial and political organizations of the working class. In terms of numbers and organization, the nineteenth-century working class could plausibly be regarded as the *rising* class. Thus Marx's nomination of the proletariat as the socialist actor was not an eccentric nomination, even if it was the product of philosophical deduction rather than empirical observation.

The point is, though, that Marx had not merely found an actor but had also written a script. The historical role of the proletariat was to overthrow capitalism and establish socialism. It would develop both the ability and the necessity to accomplish this. In performing this role it was acting not merely on behalf of itself but on behalf of the whole of humanity; and was therefore to be regarded as the universal class. It was in this form that the proletariat as socialist actor entered Marxist politics. Its entry in this form carried with it a number of significant consequences for socialist thinking. One such consequence was the socialist belief that it was not the existence of a revolutionary proletariat that was the guarantee of socialism, but rather that the necessity of socialism was the guarantee of a revolutionary proletariat. This belief sustained Marxists as they waited for the proletariat to become what it was, and enabled them to explain away the frequent postponement of capitalism's final crisis in the knowledge that next time (or the next) it would be different. When the Western working class behaved in ways that it should not have done (as in 1914), this could be blamed on the treachery of its leadership. When capitalist democracy was challenged by a mass movement (as it was in the 1930s, by fascism) this could be interpreted as marking the last stage of capitalism's crisis and therefore the prelude to socialism, even though to the untutored eye it might suggest the possibility of a movement-regime of a rather different kind.

Even though the proletariat might not look like a revolutionary class, the fact that it *was* constituted its special status. In so far as it carried the entire human project upon its own shoulders, no sacrifice was too great in its service. In the case of the syndicalist Sorel, attachment to the 'heroic' role of the proletariat as militant, historical actor even supplanted its role as the agent of socialism. Syndicalism in general, of course, looked to the industrial workers as the direct, unmediated actors of socialism, challenging capitalism at the point of production rather than through the circuitous, misleading channels of parties and parliaments. This was associated with a badge of authenticity in the form of an exclusive proletarianism: 'Pas de mains blanches, mais seulement les mains calleuses!' If it was asked how the proletariat was to develop from a class in itself to a class for itself, syndicalists would point to the class development occasioned by the general strike. Lenin, too, despite his emphasis on leadership and organization, explained how revolutionary situations overturned routine assumptions and served as a school of political education for the class of socialist actors: 'During a revolution millions and tens of millions of people learn in a week more than they do in a year of ordinary, somnolent life.'

Lenin's remark pointed to an important shift of emphasis. The proletariat would learn to play its revolutionary role *during* a revolutionary upheaval, not as a necessary prelude to such an upheaval. In other words, the proletariat retained its role as socialist actor but its ability to perform this role, even its consciousness that this *was* its role, now depended upon the ability of other actors to promote the conditions in which this class development would take place. This shift of emphasis, about which more will need to be said in a moment, directs attention to a permanent tension within the Marxist tradition on the question of socialist actors. Its origin is to be found in the need to reconcile the (philosophically) necessary role of the proletariat as socialist actor with its (actual) capacity and consciousness to perform this role. Marx described the process whereby this happy reconciliation would be brought about through the character of capitalist development itself. However, even in Marx's own writings there remains the uneasy coexistence of a proletariat enslaved by the ideological hegemony of capitalism and a proletariat expected to act as the revolutionary agent of its own emancipation. This indicated a problem, even though its existence was neither acknowledged nor explored. However, it remained as a characteristic tension within the Marxist tradition. The tension is that between the proletariat as the false-conscious dupes of capitalism and the (same) proletariat as the self-conscious creators of the new society and the new humanity.

If this tension is most evident with Lenin, it is also Lenin who confronts the problem at its source most directly. The problem is that of the relationship between proletariat, labour movement, and socialism. The working class created a working-class movement, but was there a necessary connection between the working-class movement and socialism? Such troubling questions remained hidden beneath the surface of Marx's account of the organic evolution of a class towards organization and consciousness, an account that sustained the outlook of Second International orthodoxy. It is true that Marx identified the special role of the 'communists' in providing practical and theoretical service to the working-class movement in the process whereby the proletariat developed into a revolutionary class. Their political role had its basis in the fact that (as the *Manifesto* put it) 'in the realm of theory they have over the great mass of the proletariat the advantage of clearly understanding the line of march, the conditions, and the ultimate general results of the proletarian movement'. Their special status as the most advanced section of the working-class movement derived from their superior understanding of what the proletariat essentially *was*, in terms of its larger purposes and revolutionary destiny. However, they formed no separate party of their own and 'have no interests separate and apart from those of the proletariat as a whole'.

If this might appear to raise problems concerning the role of the proletariat as socialist actor, it was not allowed to. Even if it seemed that the role of the proletariat would be acted out only with support of other actors able to prompt from the wings on the basis of their superior knowledge of the script, the relationship between these sets of actors was treated as unproblematical. For this reason Marx nowhere offers an extended account of the relationship between the proletariat and its 'advanced' section, or of the general relationship between class and party. The problem is defined out of existence by the organic, developmental way in which it makes its appearance. This unproblematical treatment is also to be found in the orthodoxies of the Second International period. It is acknowledged that the working class needs to be serviced by socialist theorists on its path to consciousness and power, but this servicing operation is treated as a natural part of an organic process of class development and is not regarded as raising any particular difficulties of its own.

All this needs to be recorded, since Lenin is frequently presented as having broken with orthodoxy in his discussion of these matters. In important respects, Lenin is able to echo Social Democratic orthodoxy in his treatment of class, party, and consciousness. Thus in *What is to be done?* he is able to cite the authority of Karl Kautsky for the latter's 'profoundly true' remarks on the relationship between socialism and the working class. As Kautsky wrote (and was quoted by Lenin):

Socialist consciousness is represented as a necessary and direct result of the proletarian class struggle. But this is absolutely untrue . . . Socialism and the class struggle arise side by side and not one out of the other; each arises under different conditions. Modern socialist consciousness can arise only on the basis of profound scientific knowledge . . . The vehicle of science is not the proletariat, but the bourgeois intelligentsia: it was in the minds of individual members of this stratum that modern socialism originated, and it was they who communicated it to the more intellectually developed proletarians who, in their turn, introduce it into the proletarian class struggle where conditions allow that to be done. Thus, socialist consciousness is something introduced into the proletarian class struggle from without, and not something that arises within it spontaneously.

Because this sounds like the authentic voice of Leninism it needs to be recorded that it is also the authoritative voice of Social Democratic orthodoxy. Moreover, it was an analysis that implied a key role for the Social Democratic party in equipping the revolutionary actor with its appropriate theoretical equipment. In Kautsky's definition, the party was the 'confluence of socialism and the working class'.

It is clear, then, that Lenin did not break new ground in arguing that class position was not a spontaneous generator of socialist consciousness, and that for such generation to occur a party and a vanguard must actively intervene. It is also the case that Lenin emphasized the need for the vanguard party to maintain close links with the workers and their struggles, an expression of the essential unity of theory and practice. Nor was it remarkable or shocking that Lenin should point out that Marx and Engels were members of the bourgeois intelligentsia, or that socialist theory generally was to be expected to emanate from this same source. Why then does Leninism nevertheless have to be regarded as an important moment in the development of socialist thinking on actors and agents, and in particular on the relationship between party and class?

The answer is not to be found in this oft-quoted passage from *What is to be done?* on the matter of working-class consciousness: 'We have said that there could not have been socialdemocratic consciousness among the workers. It would have had to be brought to them from without. The history of all countries shows that the working class, exclusively by its own effort, is able to develop only trade-union consciousness.' As has been seen, the Leninist innovation does not turn on this matter of consciousness

'from without', which was already part of a prevailing orthodoxy. What it does turn on, however, is revealed by a further
passage from the same text:

Since there can be no question of an independent ideology formulated by
the working masses themselves in the process of their movement, the
only choice is—either bourgeois or socialist ideology. There is no middle
course (for mankind has not created a 'third' ideology, and in a society
torn by class antagonisms there can never be a non-class or an above-class
ideology) . . . There is much talk of spontaneity. But the spontaneous
development of the working-class movement leads to its subordination
to bourgeois ideology . . . for the spontaneous working-class movement
is trade-unionism . . . and trade-unionism means the ideological enslave-
ment of the workers by the bourgeoisie. Hence, our task, the task of
Social-Democracy, is to combat spontaneity, to divert the working-class
movement from this spontaneous, trade-unionist striving to come under
the wing of the bourgeoisie, and to bring it under the wing of revolutionary Social-Democracy.

It is here that the balance between class and party can be seen to
shift decisively away from the class and towards the party.
Kautsky's unproblematical formulation of the class–party relationship (whatever may be thought of its merits and demerits)
had been converted into a position that might look similar but
which was now highly problematical. It was no longer a matter of
socialism and the working-class struggle arising 'side by side' and
requiring the bridge provided by the party and its theorists. In
Lenin's formulation, the proletariat left to itself would not
merely fail to develop socialist consciousness but would develop
bourgeois consciousness. In other words, this was the *natural* line
of development of the proletariat, acting as its 'spontaneous'
self, and there were no middle courses available. Thus the task of
the party was not to service the class in its necessary development
of socialist consciousness but to 'divert' the class from its natural
line of development towards bourgeois consciousness. It was not
merely the case that (contrary to the views of the 'economists')
the economic class struggle was not paramount and would not
produce a revolutionary proletariat, but that such economism
would issue in a trade-union consciousness that represented the
incorporation of the proletariat into existing society and not its
revolutionary transcendence. This was the inevitable fate of a

class untutored by correct revolutionary theory and deprived of correct revolutionary leadership.

The source of such theory and leadership was the party. It was the party that was now to determine the fate of the class. In the sense that the party still looked to the class as the socialist actor it would be inaccurate to describe this Leninist position in the language of substitutism. However, the terms of the class–party relationship had been altered decisively. The party was now to be seen as the real motor of socialist revolution, the motor that was needed to transport a class that showed every sign (if left to its own devices) of moving in the wrong direction. This had implications for the status and organization of the party. Its status derived from its theoretical credentials in interpreting and applying scientific socialism. As the carrier of correct revolutionary theory the party was the 'real' representative of the proletariat, for it was the party that knew what the proletariat essentially *was* and what was needed for it to 'become what it was'. This required a particular *kind* of party, organized in such a way that the correct theoretical perspective could be translated into effective political leadership. Such a party would not be open and pluralistic but (especially in Russian conditions) narrow, centralized, and disciplined. Thus the Leninist vanguard party of 'professional revolutionaries' was an authentic expression of a revised view of the kind of intervention that was required if the proletariat was to perform the historical role that Marx had assigned to it. It was also, of course, an indication (and an anticipation) of the authority that could be claimed by a Marxist party on the basis of its superior theoretical knowledge of the real interests of the working class (or 'toiling masses' in later versions).

Not surprisingly, Lenin's version of the class–party relationship has been challenged by other Marxists, both at the time and subsequently. The major contemporary challenge came from Rosa Luxemburg, whose charge against the leadership of the Social Democratic parties and also Leninism turned on their alleged attempt to replace the spontaneous revolutionary initiative of the class with the organized political leadership of the party. The Leninist party model was to be seen as 'no more or less than a mechanical transference of the Blanquist principles of the organization of conspiratorial groups to the social democratic movement of the working masses'. Luxemburg's attachment to 'spontaneity' did not involve a denial of the role of party, leadership, or organization; but it did involve a repudiation of any position which elevated these above the revolutionary self-organization of the class. It was the *terms* of the class–party relationship that were crucial, and it was necessary frankly to admit that 'errors made by a truly revolutionary labour movement are historically infinitely more fruitful and more valuable than the infallibility of the best of all possible "central committees" '.

Unlike Lenin (and Kautsky), Rosa Luxemburg believed that the proletariat, left to itself, was essentially revolutionary. In strikes and uprisings it gave expression to its nature and destiny. The task, therefore, was to sustain and encourage it in such self-expression, not to stifle it by seeking to force it into an organizational mould. If this view might seem to offer a rather precarious basis for a revolutionary organization (and it is possible to interpret the fate of Luxemburg's Spartacus League in this light), it could nevertheless be presented as an authentic restatement of Marx's own position on the matter. This was not merely Luxemburg's claim, but is the claim of other Marxists who resist Lenin's version of the class–party relationship. Had not Marx always insisted that (in the words of his Preamble to the Provisional Rules of the First International) 'the emancipation of the working classes must be conquered by the working classes themselves'? There could be no mistaking the view held by Marx and Engels that socialism was not merely about the emancipation of the proletariat but its *self*-emancipation. There could, therefore, be no question of confusing Marxism with Blanquism, or with Leninism. Thus a resort to the texts could provide a reassuring reaffirmation of Marxism as class action against Leninism as party action.

The only problem with such reassurance was that it returned the argument to Marx's (philosophical) belief in the essentially revolutionary character of the proletariat, instead of confronting the real implications of Leninism. Clearly a central implication was that the working class might not in practice develop a revolutionary consciousness and would require disciplined tutoring if its role as socialist actor was to be performed. In other words, the question was how the revolution was to be made *despite* the non-revolutionary nature of the working-class movement; and, a further question, how the proletarian revolution was to be made in conditions where the proletariat was not the leading element in society and economy. Lenin had confronted such questions and provided his own answers. A proletarian revolution could be engineered by a proletarian movement that was 'proletarian' in the sense that its theoretical grasp enabled it to understand the objective interests and historical role of the proletariat, even though it was not itself composed of proletarians and despite the fact that the proletariat seemed unaware of the role that history required of it and might not even exist as a developed social formation.

Thus Lenin explained how Marx's socialist actor could in practice perform its role. Moreover, however troubling the explanation might seem to the exponents of classical Marxism, it at least drew upon some relevant (if also troubling) evidence from the real world. This evidence revealed the difficulties in any attempt simply to read off class behaviour from class position, or to believe that the process whereby the latter would issue in a particular expression of the former was either necessary or straightforward. Instead of a progressive development of proletarian homogeneity and consciousness, Lenin identified a process of incorporation of the Western working class into bourgeois society and the role in this process of a working-class sectionalism in the form of a labour aristocracy and of a reformist social democratic leadership. Moreover, in identifying the character of socialist revolution in Russian conditions, Lenin not only emphasized the central role of the party as the proxy-proletariat but also identified the important role of other actors, notably the peasants and the nationalities. Furthermore, when the working class of the West failed to respond to the signal from Russia that the imperialist chain was broken (a response that Lenin's theorization of the revolution had insisted would be forthcoming, notwithstanding his own previous account of the degenerative character of the Western working-class movement), Lenin extended the cast of socialist actors to include all the oppressed peoples of the world who were the victims of Western imperialism: 'We now stand, not only as the representatives of the proletarians of all countries but as representatives of the oppressed peoples as well.'

Here, then, was the decisive moment of extension, and disintegration, of a traditional socialist cast list. The party-as-proletariat would lead the oppressed masses of the world against their imperialist exploiters in the West. Global revolution was still assured, but its agency was no longer to be seen as the working class of Western capitalism but the masses of 'the revolutionary and nationalist East'. In a significant sense the working class of developed capitalism was now to be counted on the side of imperialism, requiring a new version of emancipation from without. However, this was ensured (as Lenin explained) by the global balance of forces:

In the last analysis, the outcome of the struggle will be determined by the fact that Russia, India, China etc., account for the overwhelming majority of the population of the globe. And during the past few years it is the majority that has been drawn into the struggle for emancipation with extraordinary rapidity, so that in this respect there cannot be the slightest doubt what the final outcome of the world struggle will be. In this sense, the complete victory of socialism is fully and absolutely assured.

The denouement remained the same, but the stage was now set for new socialist actors in new roles, and in new theatres of revolution.

Thus the twentieth-century shift in the centre of gravity of socialism, first signalled in 1917 and further evidenced subsequently, carried with it a profound alteration in socialist thought and practice on the matter of agency. The vocabulary of Marxism might remain, but the 'proletariat' became a metaphor in situations where the party substituted for its absence. This was the case in China, where the Communists mobilized the peasants in a mass movement of national populism. There now exists a considerable roll-call of 'national communisms', as 'class' has fused with 'people' in assorted anti-imperialist and modernizing doctrines. Some theorists of national communism (like Fanon and Cabral) have not only substituted the poor peasantry for the industrial proletariat as the truly revolutionary class, but have also discarded Marxism in their general rejection of the Western cultural tradition. 'We looked for the working class', wrote Cabral, 'and did not find it.' It is hardly surprising that when an exponent of classical Marxism (like George Lichtheim) casts a critical eye over the ideological assortment of Maoism, Castroism, African socialism, and the rest it produces a bout of theoretical despair: 'Nationalism is identified with socialism, the peasantry with the proletariat, anti-imperialism with anti-capitalism, until all the distinctions painfully elaborated in Marxist literature for a century are cast overboard in favour of a simple dichotomy: Western imperialism versus the starving masses of the Third World.'

When Marx identified the proletariat as the carrier of socialism, it was also an identification of the kind of socialism that would be created through its agency. It was a socialism that would inherit the cultural and economic capital of the era it transcended. Thus the grounds upon which the theoretical leaders of Second International Marxism indicted the Bolshevik revolution (wrong actor, wrong time, wrong place) were also linked to a grim foreboding about the kind of regime that would result. To the extent that Marxism, in Leninist and subsequent variants, has been deployed as the theoretical (and organizational) basis of assorted popular movements of economic justice, modernization, and independence, the foreboding may be generalized into wider twentieth-century terms. Sometimes this is described as the tragedy of Marxism (nice theory, nasty world). Yet this is surely to indict the world of practice for not behaving as the world of theory decreed. Of course, classical Marxism was not distinguished by its theoretical modesty. It had solved the riddle of history, a theoretical accomplishment to be given practical demonstration through the agency of the working class of developed capitalism.

There was no difficulty, therefore, in showing why the peasantry had no role as socialist actors, or why petty nationalisms would be swallowed up by the development of the international economy and its associated class cleavages, or why the Western working class was necessarily the revolutionary socialist subject. But of course there should have been such difficulties. Something has already been said about the character of Marx's original identification of the proletariat as socialist actor, but this identification was rooted in a view of the wage-labour–capital relationship as the basic determinant of social reality through the class action it generated. However, why should class position generate class action of a particular kind? And why should a general theory about the nature of social determination provide a reliable guide to the actual forms and consequences that such determination might give rise to? More fundamental still, why should the class antagonisms associated with the mode of production be regarded as of singular, determining importance compared with the manifest antagonisms generated by racial, ethnic, religious, sexual, and other conflicts?

If such questions could be ignored by nineteenth-century Marxism, they at least have to be confronted by Marxists at the end of the twentieth century. For example, in 1848 the founders of Marxism could confidently predict the socialization of the nation; but a century later it already seemed more plausible to record (in E. H. Carr's phrase) the 'nationalisation of socialism' (and it might be recalled that Marx announced the resolution of the national question in class terms at the very moment in European history at which nationalism gave notice that it was unlikely to be content with such subordinate and derivative status). The failure of the Western working class to behave in the way expected of it has naturally been seen as a major theoretical problem, as has the ability of the party to substitute itself for the (determining) class in the Communist party-states. There has arisen a new Marxism of the 'superstructure', sometimes (as with Marcuse) with grimly pessimistic conclusions about the prospects for working-class consciousness and action, but in other hands (as with Gramsci's latter-day disciples) with a more optimistic scenario in which, serviced by its 'organic' intellectuals, a project of working-class cultural hegemony becomes possible. In general, though, the problem is still framed in formal Marxist terms as that of accounting for the disparity between class position and class behaviour. Yet in this form the problem derives from the terms in which it is discussed, and produces the spectacle of so many contemporary Marxists boxing their way out of corners they need not be in. It is possible to admire the deft footwork involved, while regretting the needless expenditure of so much effort.

In Marxist terms, much of the responsibility for the failure of the working class in the West to 'become what it is' lies with the social democratic parties and their leaderships. The charge against twentieth-century social democracy is that it has betrayed the working class through its parliamentarism and reformism and has therefore to be regarded as 'objectively' on the side of the existing order despite its ideological veneer and notwithstanding its majority support amongst the working class. This charge was first framed by Lenin (who, it might be recalled, also explained how the British Labour Party was not a proletarian party despite its actual working-class composition, whereas the Bolshevik party was a proletarian party despite the absence of the proletariat in its ranks); it became the orthodoxy of the communist parties; and remains basic to much contemporary Marxism. While it is clearly the case, to put the matter briefly, that social democracy has often shown itself prone to accept the standing invitation from liberal capitalism to degenerate into mere electoralism and a permanent accommodation with the existing order, it is also the case that (at some times and in some places) it has not merely demonstrated an ability to resist this invitation but to press some of its own definitions on to the wider society. At this point the argument becomes familiar, and always inconclusive. The Marxist charge against social democracy for betraying the working class into bourgeois reformism is met by the social democratic counter-charge that it operates with people as they are in conditions of political democracy. The argument is unlikely to become fruitful while the 'objective' role of social democracy, always and everywhere, is proclaimed as an article of faith by those whose belief in the 'essentially' revolutionary and self-emancipating capacities of the working class remains disconcertingly untroubled by the ease with which those capacities can evidently be thwarted by social democratic politicians (as well as by Leninist parties).

In important respects, of course, the social democratic tradition (in its generic post-1917 sense, which includes those non-communist and, usually, non-Marxist positions that have preferred to describe themselves as democratic socialist) has wanted to give its own account of socialism's actors. While rooted in the organized working-class movement, it has wanted to match the universality of the socialist idea with a movement that reflected this universality. Thus even during the Second International period, when Marxist orthodoxy proclaimed the proletariat as the universal class, Jaurès preferred to present the socialist party as 'the geometrical locus of all great causes and all great ideas'. Marxism had conjoined the idea and the interest, the universal and the particular, so that socialism was to be seen *as* the victory of working-class interest. Democratic socialists refused this formulation, in favour of a position that combined working-class interest *with* socialism. The universality of the latter should not be reduced to the particularism of the former. The working class, as the exploited class of capitalism, would be the main beneficiary of socialism and the basis of a mass socialist party, but it should not be identified with socialism. Such an identification would be wrong in both principle and practice.

It would be wrong in principle because socialism is at bottom a matter of values and therefore accessible to anyone capable of making a moral choice; and because the Marxist habit of dealing only in class categories left too little 'space' for individual human beings. It would be wrong in practice because of the flawed social analysis that sustained it. A united, revolutionary class of enlightened socialists was an unlikely development of a working class that had been degraded and sectionalized by capitalism. As Bernard Shaw put it, 'such an army of light is no more to be gathered from the human product of nineteenth century civilisation than grapes are to be gathered from thistles'. Moreover, it was an illusion to believe that capitalist crisis served to radicalize the working class; just as it was an illusion to believe that class polarization was underway when all the evidence pointed to increasing class differentiation and the creation of new, intermediate groupings. The conclusion from all this, on grounds of both principle and policy, was the need to construct a socialist movement of persuasion and reform capable of making a wide appeal to people in different social classes.

In Britain, the early Fabians directed their appeal to the *nouveau couche socialle* of administrators, professionals, and technicians; while R. H. Tawney, combining Fabian rationalism and socialist moralism, advised the Labour Party of the need to look less like a defender of the sectional interests of the trade unions in order to appeal to all those people 'whose business in life is not snatching at profits, but constructive activity' (though this was 'not a question . . . of giving a second place to the claims of the industrial workers, who are capitalism's chief victims, but of presenting those claims as what in essence they are, a demand for a life that is worthy of human beings, and which no decent man will withhold from his fellows'). In framing the socialist argument in this way, it was possible to tap radical and patriotic traditions and harness them to the socialist cause. Within English

socialism, for example, there has been a strong undercurrent of
sentiment relating to a 'real' England, a people's England (what
Orwell described as 'the England that is only just beneath the
surface'), and an attempt to mobilize this England for socialist
purposes. In general, then, while the communist parties have
traditionally operated within a class perspective that has issued in
a stance of workerism, the social democratic parties have sought
to combine a base in the organized labour movement with a more
generalized appeal. In its 1959 Bad Godesberg programme, the
German SPD formalized what this involved: 'From the party of
the working class the Social Democratic Party has become a party
of the people.'

However, in this particular version of social democratic
substitutism, of 'people' for 'class', the casualty seemed to be not
merely one kind of socialism but *any* kind of serious socialism. It
was not just a case of new actors, but of a different play. This
could be presented as an authentic response to the deradicalization of an embourgeoisified working class and the increasing significance of new social groups. This points attention to the
importance attached to the changing class structure of Western
Europe in contemporary socialist positions on the matter of
agency. Some socialists identified a 'new' working class attached
to consumer capitalism and drew conservative conclusions; while
other socialists found a 'new' class of technical workers raising
issues of power and control and came up with a radical scenario.
There have also been assorted attempts to find surrogates for the
traditional proletariat on the Left, though often (most conspicuously with the student 'revolution' of the 1960s) still reflecting a
belief in the need to attach themselves at some point to socialism's historical actor and sleeping giant.

All this may be taken as evidence of the contemporary crisis of
agency within socialism. Attempts to retain the 'working class' as
socialist actor, in the face of this crisis produced by its failure to
act in the way expected of it, are reflected in the attention given to
what Poulantzas has called the 'boundary problem' in socialist
class analysis. On the one hand, the boundary of the modern
working class is drawn so expansively that socialism no longer
has to rely upon the agency of the traditional proletariat. On the
other hand, the boundary is drawn so narrowly (as it is by
Poulantzas himself) that the working class shrinks to such

diminutive proportions that any socialist strategy must clearly involve alliances with other social groups. In this way class analysis carries with it direct strategic implications for socialism. Indeed, it is *intended* to, as is evident from the kind of class analysis that has been developed by Eurocommunism to sustain its position of a 'popular alliance' between the working class and other social forces. An echo of this position, based upon a similar analysis of changing class patterns, has been heard in Britain through the agency of Eric Hobsbawm, whose *The Forward March of Labour Halted?* has provided a major focus for recent strategic debate on the Left. It is scarcely surprising that, from within the Marxist tradition itself as well as from outside it, the question is asked whether the Eurocommunist position does not really mark the abandonment of socialism's self-emancipating actor rather than its retention and redefinition. Moreover, if it does mean this, does it not also mark the replacement of 'class' by 'people' and, thereby, the abandonment of the basic Marxist position concerning the centrality of the class struggle between capital and labour as the fundamental antagonism within society?

This raises problems for the orthodox Marxists, but it need not raise problems for other socialists. Unless socialism is defined in terms of the victory of a class, itself defined in terms of the relationship between wage labour and capital, the failure of that class to perform its necessary revolutionary role does not do fatal damage to the socialist project. There is no reason to expect the working class to be the single carrier of socialism. Further, there is some reason to expect that the working class (for example, in its demand for a 'right to work', or its attachment to 'free collective bargaining') will reflect and reproduce the rationality of capitalism rather than challenge it fundamentally. It is a major achievement of feminism not merely to have identified the limited stereotype of socialism's traditional actor (male, manual, muscular) but to have identified the limited character of the wage-labour–capital relationship that underpinned it. Feminism has extended and enriched the definition of the socialist project, from 'work' to 'life', and has extended the range of possible socialist actors in the process.

'One can say', writes Bauman, 'that the history of socialism has come full circle. It started . . . as an idea in search of a constituency; it has become recently a constituency in search of an idea.' The constituency consists of all those people in search of a more rational and human way of ordering society (which includes, of course, their own lives and communities) than that offered by late-twentieth-century capitalism. If this constituency has difficulty in making connections with socialism, it might be argued (and is here) that this is related to the kinds of socialism that seem to be on offer and to the traditionally limited definition of socialism's agents. When André Gorz identifies a 'non-class of non-producers' as the leading actors of a post-industrial socialism this might seem to represent the final dissolution of any coherent socialist strategy. Or it might be taken to indicate the radical implications of recasting the socialist project in such a way that a general project requires a general subject. Marx framed the socialist project in terms of a universal humanism but tied it to a single class, fighting on a single front. The crisis occasioned by the failure of this actor to perform as expected might yet enable socialism to find a base as broad as its prospectus. Moreover, as Bahro has said, 'the way leading out of the present situation need not be conceived as 'socialism' by all who want to tread it.'

7. Futures

Socialism is dead.

Alain Touraine

Socialism is only a possible future.

Tom Bottomore

The problem with being a socialist at the end of the twentieth century is that the rest of the century has already happened. If the nineteenth century taught some powerful lessons about the nature of capitalism, to set against its own self-image, the twentieth century has performed a similar service in relation to socialism. In many respects it has been socialism's century. On one view, this becomes a story of victory and vindication. On another view, however, it turns into dismay and disintegration. As Bauman describes it, in *Socialism: The Active Utopia*, 'the two centuries of modern socialism's history extend from its majestic advent in the attire of utopia to the incapacitation arising from its alleged realisation.'

Consider the contrast between the socialist world of 1900 and that of today. In 1900 there were no socialist countries, but a confident expectation that there soon would be. Both Marxists and Fabians conscripted history to their side, and presented socialism as the necessary outcome of a process of economic development. The Marxists had a comprehensive science of society which explained why capitalism was destined to collapse under the weight of its own economic contradictions and why a revolutionary proletariat would conquer power and establish a classless society. The Fabians had a historical science which revealed the drive towards collectivism that could be harnessed by reform and reformers to establish a socialist organization of production and distribution. Both Marxists and Fabians, it should be added, assumed that socialism would be constructed upon the economic, political, and cultural foundations of a mature capitalism.

Nearly a century on, things look very different. Hundreds of millions of people now live under socialist regimes around the world, but not one of these regimes even approximates to the description of socialism offered at the turn of the century by either revolutionaries or reformers. The reformist perspective, of the Western working class voting its way to socialism, seems to have ground to a halt in the shifting sands of a social democracy that has come to represent a form of welfare capitalism. The revolutionary perspective has fared even less well in the West, owing to the persistent refusal of its actors to perform their historical role. The success of socialist revolution elsewhere, from 1917 onwards, has created the authoritarian party-state as the twentieth-century representative of 'actually existing socialism'. At the beginning of the twentieth century, Marxism could present itself in terms of a universal humanism; at the end of the twentieth century it has to confront the fact that every Marxist state is a dictatorship. This may be a necessary fact (as its critics argue) or a contingent fact (as its friends suggest), but it is a decisive fact in explaining the salience that 'socialism' has come to have for the populations of Western capitalism.

At this point it would seem plausible to settle into a conclusion of the following kind. A reformist socialism has established itself as the appropriate form of socialism in the countries of capitalist democracy, but has only been able to deliver social democracy. A revolutionary socialism has shown itself to be appropriate to other societies, but only in an authoritarian form. In this sense, early-century socialists in Western Europe were correct in tying their version of socialism to general economic and social development. However, they were wrong in believing that such development would necessarily issue in socialism, whether through revolution or reform, and in disbelieving that other versions of socialism were available where their preconditions were absent. They were prisoners of their own theory, especially when they dressed it up as science, which is why the recalcitrant world of practice was capable of taking them so much by surprise.

Not merely is the conclusion just stated plausible in terms of the evident connection between kinds of socialisms and kinds of societies, but it corresponds to the twentieth-century organization of rival socialist camps. An authoritarian communism (East) confronts a reformist social democracy (West). In the socialist world cup, the match between the Soviet Union and

Sweden has been in progress for much of this century, and looks likely to continue for a long time yet (certainly in the absence of own goals or penalties). Here, then, is an important part of the twentieth-century dilemma of Western socialism. The century's lesson seemed to be that there were only two choices on the Left, between an undemocratic communism and an unsocialist social democracy. If this was indeed the choice, then it was hardly surprising that Western workers (and many socialists) should settle for social democracy and decline invitations to embark on a more perilous course. They had more to lose than their chains, and this 'more' included the political freedoms and democratic rights that they had struggled so long and hard to achieve. As Lichtheim puts it: 'social democracy might be boring, but at least it was familiar and held no menace to freedom and decency.'

The socialist credentials of the social democrats might be disputed, and the degenerative tendencies of social democratic parties in office might be acknowledged, but their democratic credentials were sound. They could therefore brush aside the guilt-by-association smears from the Right on this score, while the charge of 'electoralism' levelled against them from the Left could be taken as confirmation of their democratic sensibilities. Their commitment to socialism might be uncertain, or postponed to an indefinite future, but not so their commitment to democracy. In so far as the twentieth century had suggested at least the possibility that there might be a trade-off between socialism and political freedom (and certainly that, contrary to an earlier prospectus, there was no necessary connection between socialism and political freedom), the working class of the West sensibly preferred to err on the side of political freedom. This option was, of course, made more attractive by the ability of social democracy to combine democracy with welfare, by extracting reforms and improvements from capitalism on a continuing basis. Such reformism was already the practical policy of pre-1914 social democracy, despite its Marxist camouflage, and became the explicit basis of later social democratic politics.

It is the need to make an accommodation with the political facts of life in Western Europe that has also moved the communist parties in a 'Eurocommunist' direction. This direction is unmistakably towards social democracy, and involves a repudiation of an earlier Leninism with its dismissal of 'bourgeois' democracy. It is true that Eurocommunist protestations of faith in the institutions of parliamentary democracy, and repudiation of the revolutionary road, are matched with equally loud protestations that there is no ideological dilution of a social democratic kind involved in this process; but the *direction* of change is clear enough. If Carrillo, one of the architects of Eurocommunism, insists that 'there cannot be any confusion between "Eurocommunism" and social democracy in the ideological sphere' because the former 'proposes to *transform* capitalist society not to *administer* it', this cannot conceal the adoption of a position which at the beginning of the century would have been regarded as a clear endorsement of 'revisionism', and which at the end of the century would be echoed at the ideological level by many sections of social democracy.

However, if Eurocommunism has endeavoured to shed some of its political problems by moving in a social democratic direction, it has thereby also acquired the contemporary problems of social democracy itself. The Eurocommunists might claim that they really *mean* it when they say they are in the business of reforming their way to socialism (unlike the social democrats, who merely say it), but this by itself is scarcely enough to sustain an effective socialist reformism. If Eurocommunism is a reflection of the historic problems of the communist tradition in the West, the social democratic tradition confronts major difficulties of its own. This is why the earlier comfortable conclusion about a social democratic reformism having established itself as the appropriate form of socialism in the West turns out to be rather too comfortable. The strategy of social democracy has been to milk the capitalist cow, an activity that has continued steadily if erratically through the present century. Its fruits are to be seen in the growth of protective legislation and welfare provision that constitutes the history of social policy in this period (and which, in historical terms, represents a major advance in the security of working-class life).

In the mid-century heyday of social democracy it was possible to believe that this process would continue in uninterrupted fashion. The socialist milk would continue to flow in abundance from the capitalist cow. Indeed, upon the basis of this belief it seemed plausible to claim that traditional socialist objectives (defined in terms of welfare and social equality) could be achieved without the traditional socialist means (social ownership of the means of production). Welfare capitalism could be made to deliver the social goods that 'socialism' had traditionally stood for and which 'socialists' had formerly believed could only be achieved through the abolition of private ownership of the means of production. The *locus classicus* of this confident social democratic revisionism is Crosland's *The Future of Socialism*, written in the mid-1950s, with its admiring glances towards the social democratic parties in Germany and Sweden, where old ideological baggage was being tossed overboard (to beneficial electoral effect).

It is clear now that this position rested upon a view of modern capitalism that was too benign and domesticated. It did not take account of the dynamic of inequality within capitalism that was serving to increase inequality rather than to diminish it, even (as Titmuss showed at the time, and has been amply confirmed since) through the organization of welfare itself. In other words, traditional socialist objectives were *not* being achieved, even though there was a general increase in social welfare and living standards. Thus it was not merely a matter of revising socialist *means*, but of redefining socialist *ends* as well. This was the option taken by some social democrats, involving a historic adjustment of ambitions in the direction of what capitalism could actually deliver and the renunciation of larger purposes. The formation of the Social Democratic Party in Britain might, perhaps, be taken as a formal declaration of this kind. If capitalism could not deliver equality, then the social democrats would settle for what it could deliver and carry on milking as best they could.

This points to a fundamental characteristic, and difficulty, of the social democratic tradition in general. Much of its efforts have been concerned with making alterations to the pattern of distribution under capitalism, through an extractive politics of reform and concession. However, this kind of distributional politics has been most successful during periods of capitalist buoyancy and growth, and least successful during periods of capitalist crisis and contraction. In other words, it represents a politics of *dependency* rather than of opposition and transformation. The long post-war capitalist boom was therefore also the period when social democracy was most confident and successful, while the collapse of this period of expansion has brought with it a crisis for social democracy. Indeed, at such times the achievements of social democracy in terms of welfare provisions and protections against unrestrained market capitalism can be presented by capitalist 'common sense' as an incubus that is preventing the economic system from performing effectively according to its own internal dynamics. The logic of this argument has been deployed to good effect by the contemporary New Right in the context of economic recession, while the social democratic Left has found it difficult to mount a credible resistance or alternative when what was needed was not a dependent strategy of distribution but a convincing strategy of production.

This suggests a more general organizational and theoretical vulnerability on the part of social democracy. Its method was reform and its instrument was the state. The effect was that it piled ever more powers and responsibilities upon the state but without giving any serious thought to the organizational problems of social democracy in terms of control, autonomy, and accountability. The vision of the welfare society thus turned into the bureaucratic apparatus of the welfare state. Centralism and uniformity triumphed over decentralism and diversity. A socialism of self-government was lost in an administrative collectivism. Social ownership turned into state ownership. This is put too baldly and without the necessary qualifications, but it forms part of the current crisis of social democracy. Not merely has the extractive, distributional strategy of social democracy been disabled by economic crisis, but its attachment to the state (in circumstances where people do not experience the state as 'their' state) has made it vulnerable to libertarian arguments about freedom, choice, and autonomy. Thus, in both East and West, socialism has come to be associated with statism and bureaucracy rather than with democratic self-government, and this has produced a marked disinclination on the part of Western electorates to believe that it is desirable to extend a socialism of distribution into a socialism of production.

If all this reflects the contemporary difficulties of social democracy, it also reflects the reason why this tradition cannot stand still. If one option is to throw the towel in and make a final accommodation with capitalism, another option is to attempt a redefinition of theory and strategy. This is evident in the radicalization of social democratic parties in Europe that has taken place in the 1970s and 1980s, equivalent to the deradicalization that occurred a generation earlier. This is also why the characterization of the 'objective' nature of social democracy traditionally offered by the Marxist tradition is scarcely adequate. Indeed, Marxism's own difficulties are apparent enough. At the beginning of this century there was a comprehensive, scientific Marxism; towards the end of the century there is a whole range of Marxisms. There is both a 'revival' of Marxism and a 'crisis' of Marxism. At the beginning of the century the intellectual leaders of European Marxism were also the leaders of the Second International parties, and of an advancing political practice; at the end of the century they are the practitioners of a 'Professorial Marxism' (Parkin's phrase) of the closet and the learned journal, and of a receding political practice. Moreover, the focus of much contemporary Marxism has shifted significantly. As McLellan points out, 'whereas Marx started with philosophy and moved to economics, the typical thinkers of Western Marxism have moved in the opposite direction'.

In significant respects this century has seen the collapse of the whole pack of cards that constituted classical Second International Marxism. The failure of proletarian internationalism in 1914, followed by the triumph of Bolshevism in 1917, gave early indication that events would not bow to the requirements of Marxist science. The implications of this for Marxist theory remained for a long time unexplored as Marxism itself was appropriated by the communists and served up in an authorized version. The renewed vitality of Marxism in the West derives from its escape from the clutches of communist orthodoxy, and the infusion of elements from Marx's work that were unrecognized before 1917 (when 'Marxism' consisted essentially of *Capital* plus Engels) and suppressed after 1917. However, much of this intellectual vitality has been directed towards problems of Marxism's own making. Capitalism has not collapsed, class polarization has not intensified, a revolutionary proletariat has not emerged. How is this to be explained? Further, there is the problem of the socialist party-states of Eastern Europe, where the abolition of private ownership of the means of production has conspicuously not delivered an end to political and economic inequality and oppression. Thus contemporary Marxism is to be found wrestling with ever-increasing opaqueness with a

formulation of 'base' and 'superstructure' that retains some significant meaning to the determining character of the mode of
production, while emphasizing the role of the ideological sphere
in explaining the ability of capitalism to maintain itself without
coercion in conditions of political democracy.

Indeed, contemporary Marxism might be seen as offering its
own gloomy commentary on the prospects for socialism in the
West. Once it is acknowledged that Marx presented the most
penetrating theorization of the workings of capitalism that
socialism has produced, but in the absence of a serious political
theory went on to draw wholly unwarranted conclusions from it
regarding the future of socialism (conclusions upon which later
Marxists were to bestow scientific status), it is not surprising that
so much of contemporary Marxism is preoccupied with the failure of history to deliver the goods.

Following Lenin, social democracy has been identified as playing a key role in this process, which seems (to put it moderately)
to rest upon a somewhat exaggerated view of the ability of social
democratic politicians to mislead a class so completely about the
nature of its own real interests. More generally, the 'problem' of
the durability of capitalist democracy has increasingly been
treated in terms of the ideological hegemony of capitalism. Much
juggling with 'ideological state apparatuses' and the like has been
engaged in to conceptualize the process whereby this hegemony is
sustained. In some versions it becomes difficult to see how such
an ideological stranglehold could ever be broken (and, indeed,
some twentieth-century Marxists have delivered this final, mor-
bid verdict on the prospects for socialism).

As ever, then, Marxists continue to be able to *explain* what is
going on: for example, why capitalism is doomed, and why it is
not; why the working class is revolutionary, and why it is not . . .
This claim to superior knowledge continues to distinguish
'Marxists' from other kinds of socialists, who cannot, it seems,
see beyond their moralistic and reformist noses. Vulgar Marxists
know that the class struggle is alive and well and the socialist
revolution is just around the next capitalist corner, if only the
social democrats who are blocking the path can be pushed out of
the way. Professorial Marxism can explain why this is not,
exactly, the case. Either way contemporary Marxism in the West

seems better at explaining the world than at changing it (which, as Marx once pointed out, is really the point).

In the face of this daunting ideological superstructure, perhaps a small dose of simple-mindedness is in order. It may not, after all, really be so surprising that the electorates of the West have demonstrated an attachment to capitalist democracy and a reluctance to embrace a socialist (as opposed to a social democratic) alternative. Further, it may be that this has rather less to do with the ideological properties of capitalism than with the revealed properties of socialism. After all, it has been possible during the twentieth century to learn something about the character of the available alternatives to capitalist democracy. The electorates of Western Europe have been able to observe societies where private ownership of the means of production has been eliminated and to compare such societies with their own. They have learnt, contrary to the assurances of early-century socialists, that it is quite possible to combine socialism with political despotism. They know that communist parties that proclaim their faith in liberal democracy have also been apologists for Stalinism. The simple-minded point is that the future of socialism clearly depends upon the ability of socialists to *persuade* the majority of citizens in the capitalist democracies that they are genuinely offering more, not less, better, not worse, and that they evidence some plausible grounds for believing that they could actually deliver on their offer.

This suggests the need for socialists to devote at least as much time and energy to the task of constructing a convincing account of socialism as to the more familiar task of denouncing, analysing, and exposing capitalism. It is, after all, the nature of the *alternative* to capitalist democracy that is at issue, since there are demonstrably worse alternatives. Marx, it will be recalled, brushed aside all such preoccupations as recipe-writing for the cookshops of the future, a pointless exercise that should be left in the capable historical hands of future socialist cooks. In general, socialists have been more than ready to take their lead from Marx in this matter. This is no longer a tenable position, if ever it was. There is more that needs to be said about socialism than that it is non-capitalism. Even if some of the recipes have to be taken on trust, people rightly want to know something about the organization of the socialist kitchen and, where possible, to test the heat.

Socialism's failure in this respect has not, of course, simply been an oversight or omission. That would be serious enough, but it is made more serious because it has derived from a particular kind of analysis (again exemplified by Marxism). An argument that says that capitalism is the source of *every* social problem (even, in some versions, of every *personal* problem) extends naturally into an assumption that such problems will not, by definition, exist under socialism, or even that *no* significant problems will exist under socialism. Thus it can be claimed that the end of capitalism will also mean the abolition of the state, power, and politics ('properly so-called'), a claim that is definitionally true in the context of the theory from which it derived, has been taken literally by its adherents (most vividly by Lenin), and is simply incredible. It is a matter of some significance that socialism's dominant theoretical tradition (i.e. Marxism) has traditionally lacked any serious political theory, since politics is to be regarded as ('essentially') a matter of something else. Current Marxist wriggling with the 'relative autonomy' of the state may be seen as an attempt to get off that particular hook.

Against this sort of background, then, it is not surprising if late-twentieth-century socialism has a somewhat serious credibility problem. This may also explain why so much contemporary socialist argument seems to consist of socialists talking to, and writing for, each other in a private language, and so little of it to be an exercise in public persuasion. If there was ever a time when socialism as theory could remain unsullied and untouched by events, that time has long since passed (or should have done). There remain, of course, those socialists for whom 'socialism' stands as the unexplored and unexplorable answer to things as they are. The word is used as if it possessed magical properties capable of dissolving every problem to which it is applied. The story is told of the advice tendered by the old hand to the aspiring Labour politician facing his first selection meeting. When asked what sort of housing policy he was in favour of, he should reply that he was in favour of a 'socialist' housing policy. Ditto for education, health, the economy . . .

A socialism of this kind is incapable of learning from experience. It will go to its grave muttering its reassuring incantations ('production for use not for profit' etc.) and wondering why nobody seemed to be listening very much any more. Its conception of 'socialism' will remain uncontaminated by the experience of actual socialist states, an experience that is judged not to be 'relevant' to its own quintessential socialism or not 'really' to be socialism at all. The fact that there is not a single existing society where 'socialism' is to be found is not thought to raise any problems concerning its own pristine model. It is enough, it seems, to be a resolute anti-capitalist, whether this resolution is displayed in the form of theoretical critique or defensive struggle of a rather more practical kind. Indeed, many socialists are clearly much more comfortable in a role that is essentially negative, oppositional, and defensive. They produce volumes on the nature of capitalist democracy, but little on the character of socialist democracy. They attach themselves to industrial struggles of resistance against the economic rationality of capitalism, but in the absence of a developed account of the economics of socialism this often looks more like a defence of the past against the future.

At the turn of the century, Bernard Shaw described how the conception of socialism held by many contemporary enthusiasts for socialism was really an illusion:

If the Socialist future were presented in its reality to those who are devoting all the energy they have to spare after their day's work, and all the enthusiasm of which they are capable, to 'the Cause', many of them would not lift a finger for it, and would even disparage and loathe it as a miserably prosaic 'bourgeois' development and extension of the middle class respectability of today. When any part of Socialism presents itself in the raw reality of a concrete proposal, capable of being adopted by a real Government, and carried out by a real Executive, the professed Socialists are the last people in the country who can be depended on to support it . . .

There is, perhaps, no need for socialism to be *quite* as prosaic and respectable as Shaw's impish Fabianism might suggest. It may not really be necessary to choose to swim with Shaw or drown with William Morris. However, Shaw's point is a real one, and has at least as much force as a commentary on the condition of socialism at the end of the century as at the beginning. Indeed, it finds a direct echo in the recent discussion of *The Politics of Socialism* by the political theorist, John Dunn, with its central theme of the need for socialists to recognize that 'the best of socialist governments is, in the end, only a government'.

Yet the fact is that many socialists, and kinds of socialism, have managed to avoid the need for this sort of recognition. Socialism becomes synonymous with social harmony. Socialization of the means of production is identified with the abolition of the state and the elimination of all forms of inequality and oppression. A socialism of economic abundance means an end to the politics and economics of scarcity. The rationality of socialist planning replaces the irrationalities of the market. Collective planning coexists with producer self-management. Even human nature itself is transformed, as the new socialist man steps into the shoes vacated by the old capitalist individualism. Now the point is not so much that socialists should not believe some of these things, but that their socialism should not *depend* upon such beliefs. For example, the new socialist man is regularly discovered at moments of great revolutionary drama. Orwell discovered him (dressed in anarchist clothes) in revolutionary Spain:

> The revolutionary atmosphere remained as I had first known it. General and private, peasant and militia-man, still met as equals; everyone drew the same pay, wore the same clothes, ate the same food, and called everyone else 'thou' and 'comrade'; there was no boss-class, no menial class, no beggars, no prostitutes, no lawyers, no priests, no boot-licking, no cap-touching. I was breathing the air of equality.

It will also be recalled, however, that the main lesson that Orwell brought back from Spain was not that this was the socialist future but that it could be so quickly and mercilessly crushed by a socialism of another, more 'realistic' kind.

The point, then, is that socialists need to look as though they know their way around the world, instead of looking as if they inhabit a world entirely of their own construction. A credible socialism would take people as they (more or less) recognizably are, even while hoping for some growth in their social feelings. It would recognize that political life presents permanent problems of theory and organization, and that such problems are not simply the problems of capitalism. This would carry with it a recognition of the need for a state as the arena of collective allocation decisions, and for machinery and procedures whereby such decisions are made. It would acknowledge scarcity as the normal and continuing feature of economic life, requiring decisions and priorities in relation to competing claims on finite resources. It would not exaggerate the superior rationality of socialist economic planning, and would accept that comprehensive economic planning is neither technically possible nor actually desirable. In this respect, as in others, it would demonstrate a capacity to learn from political and economic experience, not least from the actual experience of twentieth-century socialisms. It would not, of course, pretend that it was a science, or that it could predict the future, or that its coming was inevitable, or that it had solved the riddle of history.

In fact, it might be said that socialists need to know (and to be seen to know) both more and less. They need, in the West at least, to show not only that they understand the matters just mentioned, but that they know how to construct a socialist strategy and programme that looks plausible in terms of the political and economic situation of these societies. This is more difficult than it sounds, and only socialist rhetoric makes it sound easy. Again, Dunn makes this point well: 'The most serious political doubt about socialist policies in advanced capitalist societies, a doubt now massively grounded in the experience of the populations of these societies wherever socialist politics has had any real success, is whether socialist governments do or can know what they are doing.' Yet they clearly do need to know what they are doing, if they are to convince people on a durable basis that they can offer solutions to the problems of these societies. Moreover, the setting in which they have to operate is one where capitalism will not be replaced by 'socialism' in an afternoon or a week but where, even if it is replaced at all, it is likely to involve a political process that occupies a span of historical time at least equivalent to the rise of capitalism itself; and in which, certainly when a critical point is reached, there is likely to be resistance of a most determined kind from the capitalist *ancien régime* faced with the loss of its position and privileges.

In this crucial and difficult sense, then, socialists need to know more if socialism is to have a future. In another sense, though, the credibility of socialism depends upon socialists knowing rather less than they have in the past. In part, this involves knowing less about what other people really want or need, less knowledge about their 'real' interest and more 'real' knowledge about their expressed interests. More generally, it involves an infusion of theoretical and historical modesty. At one time it might have been plausible for socialists to claim that they understood everything and could explain everything, a claim founded upon the unique distinction of having cracked the historical code. In particular, this has been the customary claim of the Marxist tradition, and certainly helps to account for its appeal during periods when historical certainty has been in short supply. In the 1930s, for example, it was widely asserted that only Marxism could explain what was going on (a bizarre claim in retrospect, given the damage that fascism and Stalinism were doing to classical Marxist assumptions), and that to be a communist was therefore to be on the side of history and progress. 'I am a communist', declared Stephen Spender, 'because I am a liberal.' That particular god has failed, of course, but the habit of thought behind it is still hard for many socialists to break. They still give the impression of knowing (or thinking they know) more about the historical process than anybody else, enabling them to explain exactly what particular phenomena (like Thatcherism) really 'mean' and 'represent', even if appearances suggest otherwise. This usually enables them to arrive at comforting conclusions (based upon their special ability to detect immanent social trends) to the effect that history is still on course even though this may not be immediately apparent to the untutored eye.

In the past, this claim to superior knowledge has been a source of strength for socialism. It is now disabling, both because it is no longer believed and because the twentieth century has taught some lessons about those who ground their claim to political power in the claimed possession of special theoretical and historical knowledge. This does not mean, of course, that socialism has not advanced our understanding of long-term social causation through its analysis of the mode of production, but it does mean that it has extended its legitimate claim to this kind of knowledge into illegitimate claims to other kinds of knowledge (about *how* shaping trends will be mediated in practice and action). Thus there were good analytical grounds for believing that the collapse of the long post-war economic boom and the associated collapse of working-class expectations would provide an important opening to the Left. So neo-Marxists could construct a scenario in which capitalism was on course for a major 'legitimation crisis'. What the analysis would have had more difficulty in anticipating was the New Right's skilful political revival of economic liberalism and the fact that in Britain the Labour Party should decide that this was the appropriate time to shoot itself. Socialists need, therefore, to evidence somewhat more understanding of such matters as historical contingency, luck, unintended consequences, and political skill than they have evidenced in the past. This requires a certain modesty; but they do, after all, have rather a lot to be modest about.

Towards the close of the twentieth century, then, socialism is not to be regarded as inevitable, omniscient, or uniform; but is it to be regarded as dead? Does it belong to yesterday rather than to tomorrow? In some respects it clearly does carry the marks of its nineteenth-century origins, as in its putative historical code-breaking, its confident progressivism in relation to social change, its pseudo-scientism, and its identification of a class formed in the heyday of industrial capitalism as the agency of change. It is not surprising that there has been some twentieth-century reckoning with elements of this nineteenth-century kitbag. On one view, this reckoning has produced fatal consequences for the whole socialist project, leaving it stranded between an authoritarian statism as the contemporary form of actually existing socialism and a Western labour movement distinguished by a negative 'labourism' organized around the defence of sectional interests at a time when post-industrial capitalism is anyway kicking away the supports of a traditional class structure. 'It may be', writes Tom Bottomore, 'that the word "socialism" has become so corrupted by its association with authoritarian regimes, with centralised planning, with the obsessive pursuit of technological innovation and economic growth, as to be unsuitable any longer to describe the objectives of movements of liberation in the late twentieth century.'

However, there remain reasons for believing that the obituary notices for socialism in the West may at least be premature. In so far as socialism began life, and found its common thread, in a critique of capitalism, there is a real sense in which socialism is still at the point at which it came in (except that the critique of capitalism has now to be coupled with a critique of 'socialism'). Unless it is believed that capitalism has ceased to be vulnerable to the arguments traditionally levelled against it, there is no reason to think that the socialist project is exhausted. In the late twentieth century, no less than in the early nineteenth century, a system of private ownership of the means of economic production and market exchange continues to lack a justificatory moral principle, and its operation continues to produce economic conditions and distributional consequences that are damaging and unequal. It continues, therefore, to be vulnerable to socialist values and to socialist analysis, and socialism remains as the pole around which an alternative system of social and economic organization can be framed. The poor remain poor and the unequal remain unequal *because* of actions taken by the rich to maintain their position. In global terms, the South stays poor *because* the North uses its power to stay rich. Both domestically and internationally, capitalism continues to solve its problems by inflicting its 'externalities' upon other people, and as an economic system it remains anarchic and unplanned. Socialism has represented the historical attempt to harness economic life to the test of social values and social reason, and there seems every reason to think that it will continue in this role for as long as people go on wanting to put their societies into a more morally satisfactory and rational shape.

Indeed, it could scarcely be argued that there is less *need* for socialism in late-twentieth-century conditions. Technological change threatens to deliver economic and social consequences which, if left to the private determination of the market, seem set to produce casualties of an intolerable and almost unimaginable kind. The attempt to manage economic and social change on this scale, involving radical redefinitions of work and non-work and their distributional implications, is both daunting and pressing. The suggestion that it can safely be left 'to the market' is genuinely frightening. The social disintegration and *malaise* of Western societies is already sufficiently acute to suggest the need for a socialism that can offer some real prospect of human community and solidarity. Beyond this, perhaps the clearest and most perilous indication of the conflict between the private rationality of market capitalism and a universal human rationality is in the sphere of the physical environment itself, where the necessity for an eco-socialism might be thought to be alarmingly apparent.

Yet the fact that capitalism remains vulnerable to the moral arguments and empirical theory of socialism, and that the need for a 'social' order to be imposed upon the operation of market capitalism can be shown to be more necessary than ever, does not by itself provide the grounds for optimism about the future prospects of socialism. The belief that it did provide such grounds has, of course, been a source of much false comfort for socialists in the past. If there is to be development in a socialist direction in the capitalist democracies of the West (where it makes more sense to think of socialism as a process than as a product), then it seems sensible to believe that this will depend not merely upon the ability of capitalism to continue to generate moral and material dissatisfactions, but also, and even mainly, upon the ability of socialists to offer a convincing and credible alternative. It is significant that it is an insistent theme on the part of the defenders of capitalist democracy that, to coin a phrase, there is no alternative. Equally significantly, in the defence of capitalist democracy it is always the democracy and not the capitalism that is defended, in a conflation designed to suggest that one is inseparable from the other. As G. D. H. Cole remarked in the 1930s, this is capitalism's best card. Even though it loses much of its force once it is remembered that, both historically and contemporaneously, most societies founded upon private property have been political despotisms, it still retains sufficient force to serve as a powerful ideological weapon.

It is able to perform this function because socialists can argue only that it is *possible* to have socialist democracy, whereas capitalist democracy is not an argument but a fact (notwithstanding its evident imperfections). While both capitalism and socialism have revealed themselves to be compatible with political despotism, only capitalism has revealed itself to be compatible with democracy and political freedom. This evidence has not gone unnoticed by the inhabitants of the capitalist democracies, including the working-class inhabitants, and has provided a powerful incentive to settle for what they have got, or at least for its social democratic version when they can get it. At the beginning of the twentieth century, socialists assured the world that socialism was synonymous with human freedom, while anti-socialists warned that it was to be identified with coercion and tyranny. It can scarcely be claimed that the rest of the century has done much to strengthen the socialist side of the argument. Indeed, the voice of the capitalist anti-socialist has been supplemented by the official voice of actually existing socialism in the denial of the viability of a democratic socialism. Both voices, of course, have a direct interest in sustaining this denial, and equally as much to fear from its practical refutation.

What all this means is that the onus is now squarely on socialism. If it was once reasonable to take socialists, literally, at their word, this is no longer so. Many of their traditional words can be seen to have sustained positions that were thoroughly disingenuous, and people now rightly demand to see the colour of their money to check that they are not dealing in a debased currency. The character of the socialist alternative on offer in the capitalist democracies therefore becomes of central importance, and socialists face a considerable task of public persuasion. They will be disabled in this task if they do not take some trouble to acknowledge that there are demonstrably different kinds of socialism, both theoretically and practically, and go to further trouble to distinguish their own kind. There are many socialisms already in evidence around the world, and quite likely to be many more, in an assortment of ideological mixtures and capable of producing different amounts of benevolence and malevolence. Socialism, as the preceding account has endeavoured to illustrate, has always been multiform and not uniform, plural and not singular; and it is therefore both more honest and politically intelligent for socialists to shout this from the roof-tops rather than to pretend that there is a 'real' socialism which exists nowhere but against which all actual socialisms are to be seen simply as a series of irrelevant and unfortunate historical mishaps.

It is not enough, then, for socialists to argue that Western societies *need* socialism. They also have to be able to offer a kind of socialism that the citizens of these societies might be persuaded democratically to *want*. A socialism of this kind would need to be both attractive in principle and credible in practice. This would seem to imply a number of ingredients: firstly, a recognition that socialism is primarily (although not only) a moral theory, capable of generating a set of socialist values that can be articulated and applied in terms of a coherent public philosophy. In particular, this would involve a convincing account of a socialist conception of equality that genuinely enlarges freedom and autonomy, while also promoting community and fraternity. A socialism that takes its stand on this basis could not regard itself *solely* as the movement of a single class, or define itself *simply* in terms of the interests of a class, or define individuals *only* in terms of class categories, since this would be inconsistent with its general humanism. In so far as socialism aspires to represent a global humanism, an aspiration that is neither absurd nor irrelevant given the situation of the planet in the late twentieth century, there is a real sense in which its interests are everyone's interests. Not only is this true in principle, but is reflected in the growth of significant movements (for example the women's movement, the peace movement, the green movement) on the radical Left alongside and outside the traditional labour movement. If one kind of socialist responds to such developments by endeavouring to interpret and compress them within the traditional parameters of the labour movement, fortunately another kind learns from them that it is necessary to enlarge those parameters in the direction of a general movement of liberation. As Claus Offe has expressed it, 'the crucial problem for the labour movement is how to become *more* than a labour movement'.

However, a credible and attractive socialism would need to have some further ingredients. Above all, perhaps, it would need to demonstrate its possession of a theory of political and economic organization that avoided mere statism. It would need to show that it knew how to abolish the capitalist form of the concentration of power and property without thereby inaugurating a new form of socialist concentration. In terms of the economy, this would clearly involve an accommodation between plan and market, in the interests both of efficiency and consumer choice, and with a range of forms of enterprise and social ownership but with a preference for the small scale and the self-managing. In terms of the political system, it would involve the democratic diffusion of power in a system of socialist pluralism rooted in forms of territorial and functional devolution, in addition to effective general mechanisms to guarantee political accountability and civic freedom. Whenever and wherever possible, consistent with general social and economic objectives, it would be an 'enabling' state, redistributing power and property in ways designed to strengthen and extend individual and group autonomy. Indeed, it seems increasingly plausible that general social and economic objectives will positively demand this sort of policy (in the direction of what André Gorz calls a 'dual society') in response to social and technological change. Utopia comes in from the cold.

Yet utopia also needs to have its feet on the ground. The kind of socialism described here does not merely have to be selected from the political shelf, but has to be constructed through political practice. If it is a kind of socialism that knows where it wants to go, it also has no illusions about the difficulties in getting there. While socialists certainly need good theory, they also have an urgent need for successful practice (and rather less 'praxis'). Ideas work through example, and many of the examples of socialism offered in this century have inflicted considerable damage on the idea. If the best argument for socialism in Britain has been the National Health Service, then the shadow of the Gulag has hung like a black cloud over the whole socialist project. Socialism badly needs more successes, in municipal socialist initiatives, in worker co-operatives, in public enterprise, and in general policy. For similar reasons, socialist parties and organizations might reasonably be expected to prefigure in their internal life the sort of procedures and relationships they want to bring to the wider society. Parties that promise fraternity but practise fratricide deserve to have a credibility problem.

Finally, in looking back over the history of socialist ideas and movements, it is in the democratic socialist tradition that the materials for the kind of socialism described here are mainly to be found. In important respects this has been a minority tradition, squeezed between an authoritarian communism and an unadventurous social democracy. As a tradition it carries the considerable historical distinction of having added 'democratic' to socialism at a time when it mattered, to differentiate itself from an undemocratic socialism. However, it further distinguished itself by preferring to describe itself as democratic socialist in preference to social democratic, when this also came to matter. If social democrats are liberals who really mean it, then democratic socialists are social democrats who really mean it. It is a tradition that has been predominantly non-Marxist, but not necessarily anti-Marxist. A further dimension to its title derives from the fact that it has been the place where those socialists who have wanted not merely to defend but to extend democracy in new directions have found a home.

In many respects the loosening of the rival socialist blocs in recent decades has widened the constituency for this kind of democratic socialism, as part of a more general opening towards neglected and minority traditions. While this is much to be welcomed, it has in some respects made it more difficult to construct a viable and coherent democratic socialist political practice. In Britain, in particular, this has conspicuously been the case, where the Labour Party has seemed immobilized by the combined effects of a vulgar labourism and a vulgar Marxism and unable to develop a democratic socialism that is both theoretically and practically credible. This kind of democratic socialism would represent a third way between state socialism and welfare capitalism. It would also demand a considerable amount of political skill and practical imagination, in both its leaders and its supporters. It would involve a long haul, with many failures and mistakes on the way, and without any assurance of eventual success or lasting victory. It would have to live on its resources. In this sense, as Aneurin Bevan explained, it is profoundly misleading to describe it as a political middle way:

Democratic Socialism is not a middle way between capitalism and Communism. If it were merely that, it would be doomed to failure from the start. It cannot live by borrowed vitality. Its driving power must derive from its own principles and the energy released by them. It is based on the conviction that free men can use free institutions to solve the social and economic problems of the day, if they are given the chance to do so.

Further Reading

The literature of, and on, socialism is vast. The following small selection has therefore been made with two purposes in mind: to enable the reader, firstly, to fill in some of the history of socialist ideas and movements only touched on briefly and glancingly here, and, secondly, to read further amongst some of the recent literature on socialism and its late-twentieth-century condition.

Anderson, P.,	*Considerations on Western Marxism* (London: NLB, 1976).
Anderson, P.,	*In the Tracks of Historical Materialism* (London: Verso, 1983).
Avineri, S.,	*The Social and Political Thought of Karl Marx* (Cambridge: CUP, 1968).
Avineri, S. (ed.),	*Varieties of Marxism* (The Hague: Martinus Nijhoff, 1977).
Bahro, R.,	*The Alternative in Eastern Europe* (London: NLB, 1978).
Bahro, R.,	*Socialism and Survival* (London: Heretic, 1982).
Bauman, Z.,	*Socialism: The Active Utopia* (London: Allen & Unwin, 1976).
Berki, R. N.,	*Socialism* (London: Dent, 1975).
Bernstein, E.,	*Evolutionary Socialism* (New York: Schocken, 1961).
Bevan, A.,	*In Place of Fear* (London: Quartet, 1978).
Blackburn, R. (ed.),	*Revolution and Class Struggle: A Reader in Marxist Politics* (London: Fontana, 1977).
Bottomore, T.,	*Sociology and Socialism* (Brighton: Wheatsheaf, 1984).
Brown, B. E. (ed.),	*Eurocommunism and Eurosocialism* (New York: Cyrco, 1979).
Carrillo, S.,	*Eurocommunism and the State* (London: Lawrence & Wishart, 1977).
Carver, T.,	*Marx's Social Theory* (Oxford: OUP, 1982).
Caute, D.,	*The Left in Europe Since 1789* (London: Weidenfeld and Nicolson, 1966).
Cohen, S. F.,	*Bukharin and the Bolshevik Revolution* (Oxford: OUP, 1980).

Cole, G. D. H., *Self-Government in Industry* (London: Bell, 1917).

Cole, G. D. H., *A History of Socialist Thought* (London: Macmillan, 5 vols., 1953–60).

Crick, B., *In Defence of Politics* (Harmondsworth: Penguin, 2nd edn., 1982).

Crosland, C. A. R., *The Future of Socialism* (London: Cape, 1956).

Dunn, J., *The Politics of Socialism* (Cambridge: CUP, 1984).

Durbin, E., *The Politics of Democratic Socialism* (London: Routledge, 1940).

Evans, M., *Karl Marx* (London: Allen & Unwin, 1975).

Femia, J., *Gramsci's Political Thought* (Oxford: Clarendon Press, 1981).

Fried, A., *Socialist Thought: A Documentary History*
and Sanders, R., (Edinburgh: Edinburgh University Press, 1964).
(eds.),

Gay, P., *The Dilemma of Democratic Socialism: Eduard Bernstein's Challenge to Marx* (New York: Columbia, 1952).

Geras, N., *The Legacy of Rosa Luxemburg* (London: NLB, 1976).

Gorz, A., *Farewell to the Working Class* (London: Pluto, 1982).

Gramsci, A., *Selections from the Prison Notebooks*, eds. Q. Hoare and G. Nowell Smith (London: Lawrence & Wishart, 1971).

Gray, A., *The Socialist Tradition* (London: Longman, 1946).

Harding, N., *Lenin's Political Thought* (London: Macmillan, 1983).

Hindess, B., *Parliamentary Democracy and Socialist Politics* (London: Routledge & Kegan Paul, 1983).

Hobsbawm, E. J., *The Forward March of Labour Halted?* eds. M. Jacques and F. Mulhern (London: Verso, 1981).

Hobsbawm, E. J. *The History of Marxism: Vol. I, Marxism in*
(ed.), *Marx's Day* (Brighton: Harvester, 1982).

Hodgson, G., *The Democratic Economy: A New Look at Planning, Markets and Power* (Harmondsworth: Penguin, 1984).

Howe, I. (ed.), *A Handbook of Socialist Thought* (London: Gollancz, 1972).

Joll, J., *The Second International 1889–1914* (London: Weidenfeld & Nicolson, 1955).

Kitching, G.,   *Rethinking Socialism* (London: Methuen, 1983).

Knei-Paz, B.,   *The Social and Political Thought of Leon Trotsky* (Oxford: OUP, 1978).

Kolakowski, L.,   *Main Currents of Marxism* (Oxford: OUP, 3 vols., 1978).

Kolakowski, L., and Hampshire, S.,   *The Socialist Idea: A Reappraisal* (London: Quartet, 1977).

Lichtheim, G.,   *Marxism* (London: Routledge & Kegan Paul, 1964).

Lichtheim, G.,   *A Short History of Socialism* (London: Fontana, 1975).

Lindemann, A. S.,   *A History of European Socialism* (New Haven: Yale, 1983).

Looker, R. (ed.),   *Rosa Luxemburg: Selected Political Writings* (London: Cape, 1972).

Luard, E.,   *Socialism without the State* (London: Macmillan, 1979).

Lukes, S.,   *Marxism and Morality* (Oxford: OUP, 1985).

Machin, H. (ed.),   *National Communism in Western Europe* (London: Methuen, 1983).

McLellan, D.,   *Marxism after Marx* (London: Macmillan, 1979).

McLellan, D. (ed.),   *Karl Marx: Selected Writings* (Oxford: OUP, 1977).

McLellan, D. (ed.),   *Marx: The First Hundred Years* (London: Fontana, 1983).

Mandel, E.,   *From Stalinism to Eurocommunism* (London: NLB, 1978).

Miliband, R.,   *Marxism and Politics* (Oxford: OUP, 1977).

Mills, C. W.,   *The Marxists* (Harmondsworth: Penguin, 1963).

Nettl, J. P.,   *Rosa Luxemburg* (Oxford: OUP, 1969).

Nove, A.,   *The Economics of Feasible Socialism* (London: Allen & Unwin, 1983).

Offe, C.,   *Contradictions of the Welfare State*, ed. J. Keane (London: Hutchinson, 1984).

Orwell, G.,   *The Collected Essays, Journalism and Letters* (London: Secker & Warburg, 4 vols., 1968).

Parekh, B. (ed.),   *The Concept of Socialism* (London: Croom Helm, 1975).

Parkin, F.,   *Marxism and Class Theory: A Bourgeois Critique* (London: Tavistock, 1979).

Paterson, W. E., and Thomas, A. H. (eds.), *Social Democratic Parties in Western Europe* (London: Croom Helm, 1979).

Pimlott, B. (ed.), *Fabian Essays in Socialist Thought* (London: Heinemann, 1984).

Polan, A. J., *Lenin and the End of Politics* (London: Methuen, 1984).

Russell, B., *Roads to Freedom* (London: Allen & Unwin, 1918).

Salvadori, M. (ed.), *Modern Socialism* (London: Macmillan, 1968).

Schorske, C. E., *German Social Democracy, 1905-1917* (Cambridge, Mass.: Harvard, 1955).

Schumpeter, J., *Capitalism, Socialism and Democracy* (London: Allen & Unwin, 1943).

Selbourne, D., *Against Socialist Illusion* (London: Macmillan, 1984).

Shaw, G. B. (ed.), *Fabian Essays in Socialism* (London: Allen & Unwin, 6th edn., 1962).

Tawney, R. H., *Equality* (London: Allen & Unwin, 1964).

Taylor, K., *The Political Ideas of the Utopian Socialists* (London: Cass, 1982).

Thompson, E. P., *The Poverty of Theory and Other Essays* (London: Merlin, 1978).

Williams, R., *Keywords* (London: Croom Helm, 1976).

Williams, R., *Towards 2000* (London: Chatto & Windus, 1983).

Wilson, E., *To the Finland Station* (London: Fontana, 1960).

Woodcock, G., *Anarchism* (Harmondsworth: Penguin, 1963).

Worsley, P., *Marx and Marxism* (London: Tavistock, 1982).

Wright, A. W., *G. D. H. Cole and Socialist Democracy* (Oxford: Clarendon Press, 1979).

Wright, A. W. (ed.), *British Socialism: Socialist Thought from the 1880's to 1960's* (London: Longman, 1983).

Index